D0853012

The Reform of Urban Schools: Schools for the Seventies

The Disadvantaged: Challenge to Education
(with Gerald Weinstein)

Making Urban Schools Work
(with Gerald Weinstein)

Toward Humanistic Education: A Curriculum of Affect
(edited with Gerald Weinstein)

Designing Education for Tomorrow's Cities
(with Milton A. Young)

Community Control and the Urban School
(with Marilyn Gittell and Richard Magat)

PUBLIC SCHOOLS
OF CHOICE

MARIO D. FANTINI

SIMON AND SCHUSTER

NEW YORK

THIS BOOK IS DEDICATED TO MY FAMILY
—*Temmy, Steffan, Todd, Brianne, Marc*
MY PARENTS—*Carolina and Mariano*
MY SISTER—*Alma*

CONTENTS

7

PREFACE

Public schools can work. That is what the pages that follow are all about. Despite the current wave of criticism leveled at our public schools, a 1972 Gallup Poll revealed that most Americans —about 60 percent—continue to be satisfied with them (12 percent had no opinion). But the 28 percent who express dissatisfaction represent a critical mass. If their educational needs are not met, they will (in their search for satisfaction) inevitably disturb the climate in the schools for everyone. The hope of this book is to offer a constructive, achievable remedy.

The solution is deceptively simple and does not dismiss or destroy our present pattern of public schooling, as some other critics have advocated doing. To do so would have repeated their traditional errors. Rather, this book recognizes that our established mode of public education is attractive to millions of parents and students and that these parents and students have a right to this type of education.

However, in a diverse society like ours, the established process of education cannot hope to reach everyone. The 28 percent also need to have their right to quality education protected. That is what sound public education in America means. Forcing everyone to conform to the established process of education does not work.

To provide each school user with the type of education he wants and needs will require *alternatives* and *choice*. The established sequence in our schools is obviously one alternative. Others can be, indeed are being, developed so that parents, students and teachers can choose the kind of education that makes the most sense to them.

Without the development of alternatives within our public schools, our present system of public education is likely to undergo even more serious disturbance. The consequences to the growth of children, the aspirations of parents, the morale of teachers, and the future of society will be incalculable.

I began this project with two colleagues, Don Harris and Sam Nash. Although we did not write this book together, I am grateful to them for their participation in developing concepts related to *Public Schools of Choice*. My own movement toward educational alternatives for public schools did not proceed systematically; only in retrospect can I connect the notion of alternatives with my previous efforts in public school reform. Here is one incident that turned my thoughts to alternative education:

One night my seven-year-old son and I drove to a local service station to fill up the family car. When nobody appeared to help us I lost patience and left. We passed several stations before I spotted a familiar, reliable one. "This is the one I want," I said.

Steffan muttered unintelligibly.

"What did you say?" I asked.

"Oh, nothing," he said. "Only I wish I could do the same thing."

"You mean you wish you could drive?"

"No, I wish I could choose a school like you choose gas stations."

"Yeah." I laughed sympathetically. "I know what you mean."
"I've got to go to school, but I hate it. I wish I could pick a
school that would be more fun."

I realized how simple and true his observation was. "Do you
really think that some schools are fun and others aren't?"

"Sure," he said. "Even at R— some guys have Mr. P and he lets
them build things and make things. They don't have to sit at
their desks and read books all day long."

Yes, that seemed a good idea to me.

At about this time, a proposal was being advanced by a group
of education reformers (Christopher Jencks, Milton Friedman
and others) that would allow families more choice in education.
This was the "voucher plan." My personal experience (the incident just described), together with another incident involving
another one of my sons (which I describe at the beginning of
the first chapter), made vouchers and choice important concerns
in my changing philosophy of education.

In the spring of 1970, while I was still with the Ford Foundation, I participated in an education conference in San Francisco.
With me was an old friend, Dick Foster, Superintendent of the
Berkeley Unified School District. At that time I was just beginning to discuss the need for educational alternatives within
the framework of public schools. Dick Foster not only shared my
interest in the concept, but undertook to consider the possibility
of an alternatives program within the Berkeley Schools, including a project called "Other Ways," which was then being developed by a friend of ours, Herb Kohl.

This meeting led to further discussions and to a Ford Foundation grant to the Berkeley Schools for work on alternative public
schools. Since then I have spent more energy on the development of this notion than on anything else, and have written a
number of articles about the subject for professional journals.

It is my hope that this book will give the reader a thorough
enough understanding of the concept of educational alternatives

to enable him or her to implement the idea for his or her own children. This book is also meant to give the imprisoned teacher a chance to develop his or her own teaching style and talents by increasing the teacher's options. And, finally, this book should give the student new opportunities to choose the educational environment that will enhance his own potential.

My gratitude to Diane Rosen for her editorial assistance. Thanks go to Donna Olszewski, Michael Quinn and Ella Robbins for their clerical assistance. I owe an unusual debt of praise to my secretary, Sally Abbott, for her tireless effort in helping to complete the manuscript.

Finally a warm word for my family who gave of their time so that I could complete this book.

And compliments to my sons, now twelve and ten, who taught me much about individual rights.

PUBLIC SCHOOLS
OF CHOICE

I / MOVING TOWARD CONSUMER CHOICE IN EDUCATION

Freedom has two essential elements: the right to choose and the ability to choose . . . an "open" society is one of open choices—and one in which the individual has the mobility to take advantage of those choices.

—PRESIDENT NIXON

Several years ago, when I lived in a predominantly middle-class suburb of New Jersey, one of my sons was having problems in school. Actually, he had been placed in first grade against the advice of the teacher and principal, who felt he should repeat kindergarten. Our protest against such retention was based on research evidence favoring continuous progress. The child began to complain about school and, after several weeks, did not want to go at all. Our sympathy and encouragement made little difference, and soon he began to bedwet. At first we thought it was general crankiness; but then, alarmed, my wife and I discussed the matter with school officials who repeated that the boy was not mature enough for first grade. We sought the advice of the school psychologist. He seemed very sympathetic to our desire for a noncompetitive classroom environment for our son, with a more supportive teacher who would allow the children to engage in all types of activities without making them feel that they had to compete with one another. The psychologist felt my

15

son would profit from a "child-centered" classroom in which competition was not part of the classroom structure. He went on to cite studies in which children given opportunities to make their own selection of foods did so without injury to diet.

Naturally, all this was music to my ears. I asked if there were any teachers in my neighborhood school who approached the classroom situation in that manner. The psychologist said that there was one, but added that although this teacher wanted to move in this direction, she had really not pursued it totally, because no "official" program had been launched to legalize such teaching. Nevertheless, I felt hopeful and approached the school officials again, asking if my child could be transferred to this classroom.

The principal said no, reaffirming that whatever she did for my child, she would have to do for others. Further, she indicated that all the teachers were the same—all state-certified and all implementing the same basic program; she emphasized again that the problem was not with the program but with the child. "Dr. Fantini, you simply must realize that your son is not ready for first grade."

At this point, I lost my cool and replied, "No, it is you and the school that are not ready for my son."

Realizing that I had cut communication with the principal, I appealed to the superintendent of schools. He felt that very little could be done at the moment, although an experimental program was being developed. Deeply frustrated, concerned about the welfare of my six-year-old, I had to make a decision either to put more pressure on him to adjust to the program that had "turned him off" or to seek alternatives.

I decided to seek alternatives. One was to investigate other public schools in the region that might have embarked on a more flexible program. I called several professors at Rutgers University who specialized in the field of "ungraded, continuous progress" education, and they suggested a school about twenty minutes from my home in a neighboring middle-class town.

I talked with the administrator of this school, and, indeed, he said, they were beginning a nongraded, continuous progress plan in which each child could proceed at his own rate. This came close to the concept of noncompetitive education I was looking for, and I said, "Well, I'd like to enroll my child here."

The principal noted my address. "You are a tuition case," he announced. "You will need to see the superintendent of schools. It is out of my hands."

Feeling even more hopeful, I agreed that the principal of the school could not determine the fees and I went to talk with the superintendent of schools.

At this meeting, which was quite cordial, the superintendent said he was very sorry he could not honor my request. If he did so he would have to do the same for others, and there would, he knew, be too many people seeking to transfer their children into this type of school.

On this occasion too, I lost my composure, exclaiming, "If they want it, why can't they have it?"

At once, the superintendent replied blandly, "That would interrupt our whole administrative organization."

The only way, then, that I, as a parent, could send my child to a school which satisfied his educational needs was to move my entire family to a new town. That would entail buying a house in the district in which this school was located. The costs alone, over $60,000, made this alternative impossible.

Another alternative I considered was to send my child to a private school, a Montessori school nearby; but the tuition was prohibitive. I had no choice but to send my child to a school and into a classroom in which he was being damaged and scarred. Moreover, our concern for the child had by now exceeded normal proportions, and he was suffering from our persistent worry. On the one hand, we were concerned with his growth and development: he might build up negative attitudes toward school and us if we put more pressure on him. On the other hand, without school, we envisioned his falling further and further behind and becoming a chronic school problem, thus creating another whole set of educational complications.

What were we to do in this situation? We tried some home tutoring, but because of the roles that both my wife and I played, this was not a consistent approach, and the problems grew. At this point, we again made an appeal to the school psychologist. We had further discussions about the possibility of starting a "noncompetitive" classroom, now somehow given the new title of "open" classroom by the psychologist.

His major point was that we couldn't start a new program for just one child. It suddenly dawned on us that there might be other first grade parents who felt the way we did.

We launched a series of koffee klatsches around the topic of a different type of classroom. Out of this series of discussions, which the school psychologist attended, we emerged with a group of parents who expressed enough interest to start a first grade class based on the concept of "open education."

An interesting problem now arose. We had four first-grade teachers, each one handling a different group of youngsters. Though we now had a group of parents of children who preferred a noncompetitive classroom, the children of these parents were scattered among the four teachers. As far as I was concerned, there was, in pedagogical terms, a "mismatch" of teaching and learning styles. The four teachers were trying to do their best, but, in essence, each was imposing her own style on a group of youngsters—a style which might make contact with some children but not with others.

Those children for whom the teacher's style was not working tended to withdraw and, at times, posed a problem for the school. The school's response usually was to classify such children as "slow" or "disruptive"—we have such a classification system in our schools. For other children, parental pressure at home literally forced the child to adjust to whatever style the teacher had adopted, whether or not that style was congruent with the child's learning style.

I now began to raise questions about whether we could match the style of teaching to the style of learning. Obviously, in this situation, hiring a new teacher for our twenty or so youngsters was out of the question. We remembered the one first grade teacher who was disposed to a more "open" style. Our proposal would not ask for more money; it would simply ask that classes remain much as they were, since many parents and students did not express any discontent. For those who *did* express need for an alternative, a solution should be provided. *Since one first grade teacher was herself willing, and looked forward to working in an open environment, we wondered why it couldn't be done.* We had all the major parties who could make it happen. We had the parent group (the taxpayers), we had a willing teacher already on the payroll; we had a psychologist to lend support. Finally, after further negotiation and under the rubric of an "experimental program," we were able to start an open classroom as an option. We discovered that many parents whose children were in this teacher's class really preferred a more formal setup. Under our proposal, these parents also had a new choice.

As an aside, let me add that the new program did work for my son. The psychologist, my wife and I all noted a dramatic change in his feeling for school. For me, the experience opened up a whole new way of looking at education; it brought me face-to-face with the concept of "education vouchers" being proposed by Milton Friedman, Christopher Jencks, Theodore Sizer, the Office of Economic Opportunity, and others.

EDUCATION VOUCHERS

The voucher approach to educational reform differs markedly from other plans of recent years, many of which have shriveled under the weight of both popular and professional resistance. The voucher idea attempts to increase the purchasing power of dissatisfied public school users, especially the poor, by placing in their hands a new type of educational opportunity. This is accomplished by issuing to parents a voucher (a certificate) worth a given amount of money, to be applied to full or partial tuition payment at a school—private or public—of the parents' choice.*

While the voucher proposals advanced by the Office of Economic Opportunity (OEO) and various other agencies often include the public school among the alternatives from which a citizen may choose, the plan is undeniably skewed in the direction of nonpublic school options. To many reformers, the public school establishment looms as an impervious bureaucracy, incapable of genuine change; to consider serious reform within the public school framework is an invitation to perilous compromise. For them, real reform must come from *outside* the system. Thus the voucher plan is most appealing to those who want to avoid the public schools.

In point of fact, we already have a sort of voucher system in public schools. Our free system of public education does give us access to a number of public schools—but not to real alternatives and consumer choice. Our task now is to develop alternatives within our public schools—this would be an internal voucher.

To my mind, using education vouchers to make options outside the public school system—the external voucher plan—is far less important, far less desirable, than creating options within the system and making these available by choice, to parents, students and teachers. I hasten to underscore that I am not minimizing the values of the voucher-oriented system in general, but am only pointing out that the public schools already have the capacity and the resources to operate such a system *inter-*

---

* While the concept of the voucher is new to this country, it is old to some European countries. For example, the Netherlands, Belgium, and Denmark have voucher systems in operation which allow the parent to choose a public or a private school.

nally. The education voucher system has provided a new way of looking at the problem of delivering quality education to consumers dissatisfied with the old system. This new viewpoint has stimulated public schools to develop educational alternatives themselves. In so doing, the external voucher plan has actually encouraged the development of alternative public education—a constructive movement that does not demand the creation of still another expensive bureaucratic regulatory agency. The voucher emphasis on alternatives has thus given the public school establishment a new direction. I repeat, *We already have a voucher system: it is called public education. What we do not have are alternatives and choice.* Both the voucher and alternative public schools rely on increased consumer interest in optional forms of education and acknowledge the intrinsic value of individual choice. This book supports the alternative public school system, otherwise known as *Public Schools of Choice.*

It may seem ironic to advance a plan of reform within the framework of public schools when the public schools themselves have been so fiercely criticized in recent years for their intractability. Why should an alternate schools plan escape the fate of earlier reform proposals? In addition to the fact that the vast majority of Americans attend public schools (about 85 percent), there are other considerations which favor public schools.

First, I must underscore the pressure that the current and growing trend toward public accountability is exerting on public schools. Faced with the spiraling costs, the citizen, through his elected officials, is demanding a new accountability. Are the federally supported programs in education working? Are there really payoffs from the financial investments in schools of the 60's? Reports from the field on programs such as Title I of the Elementary and Secondary Education Act of 1965 are far from encouraging. Added to this new demand for public accountability is the growing awareness that add-on, compensatory approaches to school improvement usually result only in a slightly more elaborate investment in the old forms—the very forms which are being criticized by growing numbers of students and parents—that is, by the consumers themselves.

Further, citizens are defeating school budgets more frequently than in past years and are asking for increased productivity from the schools. As Americans recognize the crucial importance of quality education to their own survival, the quest for improved education continues: enter the education vouchers. Of immediate interest to the poor, the voucher has appeal also to other groups —especially to parochial school affiliates. The voucher plan, as embraced by the Office of Economic Opportunity in Washington, is a vehicle for improving the education of the poor. An OEO pamphlet on vouchers, issued in April 1972, states:

Since December, 1969, the Office of Economic Opportunity has been working with the Center for the Study of Public Policy of Cambridge, Massachusetts, to devise a system which would:
—Give poor parents greater influence over the education of their children, and greater choice among the types of education available.
—Foster educational innovation both within the public schools and outside the public school system.
—Make schools more accountable to parents at all income levels.
The study evolved from a general concern by OEO that while our public schools are probably performing better today than at any time in the past, they are not meeting the educational needs of the poor. Study after study has indicated the general failure of existing remedial and compensatory programs for the poor. At the same time, the poor, perhaps more than any other group in our society, must depend on public education for future success in life.
One means of improving the education of the poor may be the education voucher system devised by the CSPP and OEO. Under this system, all parents in the community, regardless of income, would be given vouchers with which to purchase their children's education at the school of the parents' choice . . .*

* A Proposed Experiment in Education Vouchers, Office of Economic Opportunity, OEO Pamphlet 3400-8, April 1972, p. 1.

However, the notion of vouchers has triggered a wave of professional and lay resistance. To many, vouchers are viewed as an attempt to weaken the public schools. The resistance has become so pronounced that OEO-sponsored feasibility studies on voucher education have been defeated in such communities as Rochester, New York, Gary, Indiana, and Dayton, Ohio. The attack against vouchers has been led by the National Education Association and the American Federation of Teachers. Without the support of teachers, parents and students, the voucher plan is doomed politically.

Developing alternatives within public schools should minimize this political reaction and appeal to the individual teacher, parent and student.

Traditionally, educational decision-making has filtered downward, from its origin in the obscure heights of district offices, state departments, and even federal buildings. In a large city, it is illogical that educational decisions made by one person, or a small group of persons, should ultimately influence the educational concerns of millions of individuals—parents, students, teachers and administrators alike. Yet this is what often happens. Meanwhile, parents, students, teachers and administrators, who should be natural allies working together on a common goal, expend their energies indicting each other for the shortcomings of the educational process. When the smoke clears, we are still confronted with the need for a reformed public school system which can utilize constructively the direct, unified participation of parents, students, teachers, and administrators—those closest to the actual learning process. Those farthest from the learning process are now the ones making the decisions.

In principle, the individual is the basic unit of a democratic political system. But in our highly complex society, most political decision-making is delegated to elected representatives—although the voter can, theoretically, reclaim the right to make decisions. America has seen both forms of democracy: direct participation (the town meeting) and representative participation (the Congress). Unfortunately direct participation is now often considered an anachronism.

When any institution no longer serves the interests of the individual, he has the right of political redress, as reserved for him in the Declaration of Independence. The principle of majority rule (for purposes of unanimity of action) seems a fair means of political decision-making, but it does necessarily neglect minority interests. In our society, it is pretentious to assume that any group of representatives can consistently satisfy the needs of every citizen, and this is especially true in education. Inevitably, majority rule is applied to expedite decision-making, and dissatisfied educational consumers are no longer a quiet minority. In certain quarters, they comprise a "critical mass" of concerned citizens with specific demands. For example, in New York City, consumer demand reached a stage where the structure of the city school system had to be dramatically altered through decentralization. Under decentralization, a community-based decision-making level of organization was established which cut across a highly centralized, professionally dominated bureaucracy.

This climate of no-nonsense accountability has bolstered a new awareness among those inside the public schools, the professional educators themselves. And awareness can lead to responsiveness—especially if proposals for reform are viewed as "constructive," that is, as plans in which the professionals can participate, plans which do not render them impotent.

There are many teachers, supervisors, and administrators who feel constricted by the "system" of public schooling, who are eager to connect with parents and students in a search for reform. These professional educators have been waiting for a new framework for action. In fact, many have themselves been successful in bringing about changes, at times against major obstacles.

Institutional orientation for most of the educators who work inside our public school systems has been in terms of the *current* structure, the *current* educational process. The so-called educational establishment has directed its tremendous energy and talent to trying to make the standard educational approach (age-graded organization, self-contained classes, coverage of classical content, etc.) work for every child. The problem now is that we are in an age of compulsory universal education. Diversity—cultural and stylistic—has come to overload the standard process of schooling. Professional attempts to get the learner to adjust to the school and its process have produced a system of human classification which is dysfunctional to the very aims of education itself. We have, for example, labeled certain learners "slow," "deprived," "disadvantaged," etc. But we are now recognizing that classifying people inevitably generates a psychology of expectations with self-fulfilling consequences—that a way of classifying human beings is a way of thinking about them. When we label someone "slow," we tend not to expect very much from him. The student also perceives himself to be "slow," and that perception of himself affects negatively his motivation, aspirations and sense of self-worth.

But now enough members of the public school establishment have embraced the judgment that our institutions are themselves deficient to sustain an internal effort at creating new ground rules for professional action. Professional energy can, we believe, be channeled toward developing alternative forms of education within the basic framework of public schools.

PROTECTING THE PRIMARY AIMS OF EDUCATION

Public schools have gone through a number of important stages to insure a nonsectarian, non-exclusive status that reflects the basic values of an open, free society. Public schools are mature enough, strong enough to withstand any pressures that might attempt to compromise these values—pressure, for example, to establish a Nazi school, a sectarian school, a school that portrays all whites as blue-eyed devils or a school that deliberately segregates by race or by socio-economic status. The point here is that public schools—subject to public accountability as they are—are more capable of representing our noblest values than many of our more exclusive private schools.

Moreover, alternative forms of education, to be legitimized within the framework of public schools, must satisfy other important standards. One criterion in particular deserves mention here. To be acceptable in a public school, an alternative must be capable of addressing itself to a *comprehensive set of educational objectives*, not merely to one particular set. For example, some may advance a "free school" option * based on the theory that it is complete freedom of the learner that is important—and that happiness is a major objective of education. This alternative cannot be legitimized by public schools at this time because its emphasis is on one particular objective at the expense of others. Public schools have a responsibility for a wide range of objectives, for instance:

1. Basic learning to acquire skills—reading, writing, communications, inquiring, analyzing, etc.
2. Talent development—developing individual creative potentialities.
3. Preparation for basic success in assuming major societal careers as parent, consumer, citizen, self-developing individual.

If one wishes to do so, one can categorize these aims as cognitive (intellectual) or affective (emotional); but, however classified, they remain broad at their base. Since public schools are instrumentally related to the fabric of society—involved in it,

* For a comprehensive review of free schools, see Graubard, Allen, *Free the Children*, Pantheon Books, New York, 1972.

that is, economically, politically, and culturally—it is difficult, if not impossible, for public schools to ignore or dismiss their ties to society without reneging on their public responsibilities.

Public schools must also be manpower institutions. Unless a person is independently wealthy, he must hope school will open options for him in the career market; unless a learner expects to secede from participation in society, he expects schooling to help him acquire the skills he needs to participate effectively as a citizen.

Now it is possible for certain alternative forms of education to produce people who are happy, even joyous—but who cannot read or write, or qualify for any realistic economic career. It is true that in the name of "humanistic" education, certain educational options may be overemphasized. In that case, the learner who selects these options may realize too late that he has overlooked other requirements for full involvement in the multi-environments (economic, political, cultural, social) of modern society. Ironically, he may then find that the options that so gratified him while he was in school, in the end leave him unhappy when he is denied opportunities in the real world. Public schools with their traditions of experience are more likely to protect the next generation from these pitfalls than are the less accountable alternative private schools.

If my assumption is valid—namely, that the present public school educational process constitutes but one road to a common set of objectives, and that a diverse consumer society is right in demanding alternatives to that road—then the basic problem is really the creation of valid, legitimate educational alternatives. In supply and demand terms, we now have a high demand, but a limited supply. The voucher plan is a proposal which assumes that demand will affect supply. But we have had some experience with similar efforts in other fields. For example, opportunities offered by Medicaid and the GI Bill (new demand) did relatively little to create new or more relevant health and education programs (supply). What did happen was that already *existing* alternatives were made more available to the consumer. Under a voucher plan for education, private schools would certainly benefit. New private schools would undoubtedly spring up, but of what quality? What is to prevent a slew of fly-by-night institutions from emerging during high-demand/low-supply periods? How can we assure ourselves of legitimate educational alternatives? The public schools have the manpower, the machinery, and the knowledge to deliver a new system of *safeguarded* options.

CITIZEN EDUCATION

For any educational-alternatives plan to succeed, enormous attention must be given to parent and citizen education. Unless parents and their children have basic educational information and understanding, their ability to make wise choices will be seriously curtailed. The heart of any voucher approach is individual choice among available educational alternatives. This means that parents and students, as well as staff, need to know the theory and practice surrounding each educational alternative. This type of consumer education cannot be left to chance. A process must be developed for reaching most parents and students. Here again it appears that the public schools would be better able to deal with so massive a task than the private schools.

Public schools can reach almost all learners and their parents very readily, for example, by student assemblies, parent meetings, and so on. They already have a built-in mechanism. They also have the manpower, the office-machinery and the materials needed to educate the consumer. Indeed, the task is one public schools might do well to take on, given the consequences to the schools posed by an external voucher plan. Further, certain private school alternatives can eventually be brought into the public schools; alternatives can start out as "external," and later become available as part of the public school alternatives system.

THE POLITICS OF ACCEPTANCE

Finally, there are crucial political considerations. No change in public affairs escapes politics. As we have indicated, the voucher plan has posed a great threat to the professional educator, for the voucher is viewed as a plan to bypass the public schools. Naturally, professional educators and their organizations have taken a stand in opposition to the voucher plan. As a "power bloc," educators and their professional organizations—NEA, AFT, AASA, etc.—lobby against vouchers because they threaten the survival of public schools.

The majority of Americans still attend and support a system of public schools, and they may perceive the introduction of vouchers as an attempt to weaken the public schools and strengthen private schools—including what in effect is the highly controversial funding of parochial schools. For example, this appeared in the Catholic publication *The Liguorian:*

Parents, are you tired of hysterical headlines about teacher strikes, school closing, vandalism, and school violence threatening your children? Do you feel helpless about it all, as if there were nothing you can do to control events?

Millions of lower-income parents want the freedom to send their children to the schools they think are best for them. Angered and distressed by the public schools' monopoly on community educational funds, several parents in Missouri have taken the first step. They have filed a suit in Federal District Court in St. Louis asking for equal protection of the laws for their private school children and for the parents' human right to direct and control the education of their own children in the schools of their free choice. The plaintiffs are ordinary middle-class American citizens who seek their human freedoms and the pursuit of happiness.

Bob and Mary Brusca have had it up to here in trying to pay off their modest suburban home with its yearly school tax increases. And their five children can tell you how it feels to trudge along the dangerous highways to get to their parochial schools, while their public school friends ride safely by them on the tax-paid buses. Bob first became interested in the school issue when he read of the refusal of the State Board of Education in Missouri to allow handicapped children who attend parochial school to receive needed educational therapy, such as speech correction, training for the deaf, remedial reading, and other services provided by the public schools. He joined Citizens for Educational Freedom, a parents' group launched in 1959 for the purpose of promoting laws that would end discrimination in various areas of education. Mr. Brusca asks: "Where are the 'equal opportunities' which our public school lobbyists are continually boosting when they ask for higher and higher taxes?" *

In Denmark, where the citizens are free to select either a parochial or public school, only a third select public schools. But American citizens are not likely to sit by and watch an external voucher plan, such as is envisaged by *The Liguorian*, take serious hold. Their support is clearly for an internal voucher plan.

Carried to its logical conclusion, we believe, a voucher plan would produce a parallel-school approach that could reduce the scope of public education, if not dispense with it altogether—a consequence with devastating implications for the society itself. The establishment of enough private schools to handle significant numbers of poor children alone would require major public support and, in effect, establish a private system of publicly supported schools. Middle-income parents would demand similar privileges. For financial reasons alone, the parallel-school approach is hardly likely to become widespread in the foreseeable future. Moreover, the scheme would founder on political, if not on constitutional, grounds.

These arguments are, of course, no reason to discourage pro-

* "Let's End the School Problem for Parents" in *The Liguorian*, January 1971.

grams that enable more low-income pupils to attend private schools. Private schools should continue to flourish and to offer their important options to many Americans. But there is a limit to their usefulness as an alternative to public education, for they could not serve the majority of our children, neither the poor, nor, for that matter, the affluent.

Education vouchers and Public Schools of Choice add important economic and political considerations to educational reform efforts. By placing a new type of purchasing power in the hands of the consumer, the voucher plan lets us look at the delivery of educational services in terms of supply and demand. That is, parents would be viewed as consumers with the right to demand quality services and to be provided with access to those services. Alternative public schools accomplish the same thing without as much political strife.

What, then, would the Public Schools of Choice plan be? What are its important features?

II / PUBLIC SCHOOLS OF CHOICE

*Nobody is going to argue against his [Nixon's] defense of
independence, order, self-reliance, honest work, fair play, law,
justice, the family, and clean air and water; but on how these
desirable things are to be achieved, the nation has always
been divided, and is still deeply divided today.**

—JAMES RESTON

It is important to describe what the alternatives plan "Public
Schools of Choice" is *not*. It does not resemble any of the present
options. I am not suggesting a new classification system, or
special classes, drop-out centers, or even vocational education.
As we have suggested, classification of learners is the method we
have applied in the past to provide "options" within our *conventional* public school system, but classification leads to a differentiation based on status. "Academic" programs are considered
superior to others. Students in all other categories are evaluated
as "less capable." Within the academic groupings there are further subdivisions: fast, average, slow, for example. All of these
classifications communicate to teacher, parents, and students a
scale of superiority. This system identifies even very young children as "fast," "average," "slow," or—as we may label them to
disguise our judgments—"blue," "green" and "yellow"—and the
significance of these groupings is grasped early. This leads to
potentially damaging self-perception: "I must be stupid if I am
in this group."

* "Nixon: Ends and Means," James Reston, an editorial in *The New York
Times*, January 21, 1972.

33

Also, the Public Schools of Choice plan is not the same as the "free choice" or "freedom of choice" plans whose purpose is to obviate mandated desegregation. In certain communities, court-ordered desegregation has triggered the development of special all-white schools. The term "free choice" is misleading in these cases, for the issue is basically racial. The factors of education, personnel, and curriculum are largely ignored.

The word "public" in the title Public Schools of Choice is crucial. The plan proposes a new framework for our *public* system of education. A Public Schools of Choice system would strongly encourage all parents, students, and professionals to participate in the design, development and implementation of teaching and learning environments that best meet *their* definition of quality education. Each alternative educational environment must, however, adhere to principles basic to public education in a society striving to be free, open, and democratic.

EXPANDING EDUCATIONAL OPTIONS FOR ACHIEVING COMMON ENDS

It is reasonable to assume that most, if not all, Americans desire "quality education" for their youngsters. On this, teachers, parents and students are united. When black people demanded integrated schools, they did so in order to get quality education. When private and parochial schools were established, they were instituted in a quest for quality education. "Quality education" has become a phrase which represents any education people *feel* is, or ought to be, "good" education within any school or school system. Because American society is diverse and pluralistic, it is not only appropriate, but necessary, to have various concepts of "quality education." However, as suggested earlier, an open and free society also has a *common* set of goals or objectives which represents its most cherished values and ideals. For example, a free society that values the worth and dignity of the individual must establish institutions which reflect this national purpose. Schools, as society's most basic, if not, in fact, its most strategic, institution, are expected to create conditions which maximize the value of the individual. If a citizen were asked to select the educational goals appropriate to a universal definition of quality education, he would probably agree that a quality educational program should help every learner to acquire:

1. The greatest possible understanding of himself and an appreciation of his worth as a member of society.
2. An understanding and appreciation of those persons belonging to social, cultural, and ethnic groups different from his own.
3. Mastery of the basic skills in the use of words and numbers.
4. A positive attitude towards school and towards the learning process.
5. Habits and attitudes associated with responsible citizenship.
6. Good health habits and an understanding of the conditions necessary for the maintenance of physical and emotional well-being.
7. The opportunity and encouragement to be creative in one or more fields of endeavor.
8. Understanding of the opportunities open for preparing oneself for a productive life and the ability to take full advantage of these opportunities.
9. An understanding and appreciation of human achievement in the natural sciences, social sciences, humanities, and the arts.
10. Preparation for a world of rapid change and unforeseeable demands in which continuing education throughout adult life should be a normal expectation.*

American public education has systematically developed a massive, uniform, monolithic system for achieving these common objectives. Alternative routes to these common objectives are indeed available to parents and students, but, for the most

* Melvin Tumin, "Ability, Motivation and Evaluation: Urgent Dimensions in the Preparation of Education," in *Needs of Elementary and Secondary Education for the Seventies: A Compendium of Policy Papers,* compiled by the General Subcommittee on Education of the Committee on Education and Labor, House of Representatives, Ninety-First Congress, First Session, March 1970, pp. 775–6.

part, only *outside* the public schools, Alternatives *within* the public school framework are available only infrequently and often only by *chance*. The options inside the standard public school model depend mainly on personal factors—the strength or sensitivity of a particular teacher or administrator. If a student is lucky, he connects with a good teacher. The next semester he may not be so fortunate. If the parents decide that they would like their child to be taught by another teacher than the one he is assigned to, they usually find administrative opposition; the present educational ground rules can rarely deal adequately with such demands without serious consequences to the normal operation of the school (e.g., the administrator must support his teachers or face staff morale problems).

In most school systems, regardless of their size, some schools invariably have better reputations than others. The "better" schools are usually those associated with the prosperous sections, whether or not they have modern facilities. These desirable schools appeal to most teachers both within and outside the system. Real estate agents mention them in their ads. Other schools strive to emulate them. Parents want their children's schools to offer the same facilities, the same equipment, the same books and materials as the "better" schools in the system. In many cases, equalizing expenditures and instructional procedures has been an important step. However, it has sometimes also undermined the notion of educational diversity within the system. Sameness has lead to uniformity and unresponsiveness to individual differences among students and teachers.

It is doubtful that any American would oppose a school that valued the individual, believed in human dignity, or aspired to develop good citizens. These are common goals that become the subject of controversy *not* when they are stated as ends, but only when the *means* for achieving them are implemented at the individual neighborhood school level. Thus, it is at the implementation level that common goals become controversial. It is when a school or individual schoolteacher attempts to define a goal in a manner considered incongruous with the ideas of the majority in a particular community that opposition arises. If teachers consider the teaching of citizenship important, they may become foci of controversy when they discuss the actual *behavior* of the good citizen. Controversy may arise, too, when a teacher and his school undertake to practice citizenship by protesting social conditions that limit the rights of the individual —when for example, a response to social injustice takes the form of a demonstration in front of City Hall to protest failure to enforce housing codes.

When the goal of citizenship is thus defined in action, parents and other community residents may object to the *practice* or *behavior* of the teacher, or even to the concept of good citizenship as set forth by the teacher. They may feel that good citizens do not protest in that particular manner, or that their public schools should not handle the teaching of citizenship as an act of direct participation, or that teachers should not assume the stance of social action. They may believe teaching good citizenship ends with study of a book on "Principles of Democracy," or with discussion of basic social questions. Similarly, the common goals of "human fulfillment" or "developing human potential" will kindle little controversy—until devices are established to implement these goals. Thus, regulation of *behavioral practices* in relation to common goals is a process that *must* be initiated and worked out on individual school and community levels, if dissension is to be avoided.

If a teacher or principal individually initiated a program of "sensitivity training" in which students engaged in open, unlimited, direct dialogue with each other, parents and other community residents might well raise strong objections. The *process* by which commonly accepted educational goals are subjected to community approval is at the center of several dramatic cases in the history of American education. One such case is the

Pasadena story, in which the superintendent of schools and his professional staff attempted to implement "progressive" educational programs as a new means to achieve established goals. In that instance, the majority of the community objected to the programs and ultimately demanded and received the superintendent's resignation.

In our society, any definition of quality education must also include specification of the *process* by which common goals can be implemented. This means that no group of professionals or lay citizens can *impose* on other groups programs which they do not fully understand or embrace. The importance of process is often overlooked in our highly complex and specialized institutions.

Those who possess expertise in particular areas, such as professional educators, may feel that the responsibility for the planning and implementation of certain programs has been delegated to them, and that this process does not include consumer participation, but should rather, on the other hand, include an assembly of the most skilled professionals to plan the "best" programs for the total community. Several dramatic examples, however, have underscored anew the importance of consumer participation. In New York City, the unveiling of a bold, visionary master plan for the city was greeted with severe criticism because some felt the plan had been developed in exclusion of the black community, and did not include representation and participation of that group.

Even if a plan or program were objectively evaluated as "in the best interests" of the recipients, it might still be rejected if the recipients were not themselves involved in it—had not themselves contributed to its development. For that reason, at the neighborhood or school level all plans and programs must be sanctioned by the "recipients." If their participation includes decision-making, the process stands a stronger chance of succeeding. The cry for community control of schools or, more accurately, the struggle that the minority groups and the poor are waging for self-determination in their schools, is in fact an expression of the need of the people of a community to participate in the fundamental decisions that affect their lives. In our society, final decision-making authority does purportedly rest with the people. We aspire to develop a highly informed populace, so that when decisions are made, citizens in a variety of communities and positions can assume their right to participate in the process. One of the most important areas for individual participation is the public school. However, those who aspire to influence the schools must be answerable *to the elected officials* who govern the local schools—i.e., to a political process based on representative government. While the tactics of local control, decentralization and community control do increase the voice the community has in educational affairs, they do not guarantee that *each parent, student or teacher* can make decisions (or have options) or that the decisions of the elected representatives will reflect the desires of *each* constituent.

TOWARD INDIVIDUAL DECISION-MAKING

The Public Schools of Choice model would provide the *individual* parent, student and teacher with direct choice among alternative education forms—those now in existence and others yet to be developed—all *within* the framework of the public educational system. Let us illustrate: one set of universal educational objectives has to do with mastery of the basic skills and academic proficiency. The means for achieving these objectives is the standard mode presently offered in public schools: the first grade is followed by the second grade, the third grade, and so on. Students who do not proceed according to the age-grade norms may be compelled to repeat the grade; standards are established on the basis of these norms. Children compete for rank in their marks. Various types of subject matter are clearly covered during the day—reading, science, history, etc. Since most of us are more familiar with this type of education than with any other, most parents, teachers and students may rightfully opt for it.

One alternative to this standard program is the "open classroom," popularized by such books as *Crisis in the Classroom,** and *The Open Classroom.*† In this scheme, the learner proceeds at his own rate, in an informal classroom setting. Children of different ages may be grouped together in a type of family grouping. There may not be age grades at all. How can this option be offered to the parties of interest? The "open" alternative may be known to only one of the parties of interest, the professionals. Awareness of such alternatives is conventionally achieved by reading professional publications and attending professional conferences, and these experiences are more available to administrators than to teachers. Most students and parents have no direct access to professional matters. Consequently, those farthest from the action are those most knowledgeable about this alternative. Teachers, students and parents, the closest participants—and thus those who most need access to knowledge of alternatives—are the ones least likely to be aware that alternatives exist.

A system of Public Schools of Choice increases awareness of alternatives at this basic, grass-roots level. In the case of the "open classroom" alternative, teachers, parents, and students would have the choice of continuing in the standard pattern or developing an "open" system. If, in a particular school, 10 percent of the parents, students, and teachers felt they would like to explore an open classroom system, they would have that right. Under existing circumstances, either the 90 percent overrules the 10 percent, or the 10 percent tries to impose its choice of an open pattern on the 90 percent. It's all or nothing on both

* Charles Silberman, *Crisis in the Classroom.* New York, Random House, 1970.
† Herbert Kohl, *The Open Classroom.* New York, Vintage Books, 1969.

sides. Under a Public Schools of Choice system, both would have their programs implemented. This point deserves further explanation. Under the present structure, a program develops when a new educational approach is embraced by a particular group: parents or teachers, or a combination of the two. A struggle develops in which a group tries to change the educational program of the school by imposing its new approach or format on those who may be perfectly satisfied with the existing program. In such cases, a conflict usually results as to which is the "best" educational means.

But the new approach, in contrast, *could* be implemented side by side with an existing program, providing parents, students, and professionals with at least two alternatives from which to choose. The choice process legitimizes various options, *each* geared to the common set of objectives. Alternative approaches need not take place at different schools; they can exist within a single school. If a plan for an ungraded class were proposed, those teachers, parents and students in the neighborhood schools who are *attracted* to this form of education would be free to formulate and implement it in a "school within a school." People have a right to their choice. What this choice process does is not only to legitimize the alternative, but also to make it operational, to make it a *behavioral specimen*—something people can "see," and "touch"—something that educates the other parties of interest. If an "ungraded" or "open" alternative proved more effective than the graded pattern, more' students and parents might choose this method, not by imposition, but by informed choice.

THE GROUND RULES FOR PUBLIC SCHOOLS OF CHOICE

To get any new system to operate, the participants must agree on ground rules. To make Public Schools of Choice work, its ground rules must be clearly defined. One ground rule is that *no alternative within a system of choice can practice exclusivity.* No child can be excluded from any school or alternative solely because of race, religion, financial status or—within reason—the nature of his previous educational background. The schools must be truly open, able to survive on the basis of their educational merits and their ability to meet the needs of the students and parents they serve. A school and its programs must be able to educate *all* the children—not just white children or black children or average children or "gifted" children.

Another ground rule is that each school must be working toward the *comprehensive set of educational objectives* (as stated earlier). These objectives or educational goals must be common to all schools within the system of choice. They should include mastery of the basic skills: reading, writing, English, and sciences; nurturing of physical and emotional development; vocational and avocational preparation. The student must be equipped with a broad range of skills so that he will have many choices— as many alternatives and opportunities as possible—for social and educational mobility. Within a system of Public Schools of Choice, the real issue is not what goals to set, but *how* best to achieve the goals set. The system itself seeks out options, new means of increasing the chances for the student to mature as a maker of choices, not a mere victim of circumstances.

A ground rule intrinsic to the idea of a free and open society and, therefore, to the notion of Public Schools of Choice, is that *no educational plan or design can be imposed.* Within a system of choice, the alternative schools and educational situations are presented to the consumer and, as in a supermarket or cafeteria, the *individual* "shops around," chooses, selects, tests, and finally settles on a school or learning environment that appeals to him. If 90 percent of the consumers settle on approach A, and only 10 percent want approach B, then 90 percent of the system's schools provide approach A and 10 percent approach B. Similarly, if there were a 50-40-10 percent split among choices X, Y and Z, the schools and their programs would have to be arranged according to that distribution. Each community would have to determine how many consumers were necessary to warrant a change. The point here, however, is that once the minimum percentage was established, the individual consumer—student or parent—could choose "his own option," rather than be forced into accepting one because there were no alternatives.

Obviously, new approaches will necessitate the retraining of teachers, but this can become an integral part of the staff development program of the school district.

Another ground rule is that *each new alternative must be developed and able to operate on a financial level equivalent to the per capita cost of the school district as a whole.* Although each new option may be permitted some additional costs for initial planning and development, within a reasonable period of time it must conform to the standard per student cost of the total system. We propose this ground rule to insure that there be no additional or increased costs for a public school system of choice, but rather a *wiser, more productive use of existing monies.* Within the framework of a choice system—and of a free and open society—all people, regardless of economic means, should have choices.

The public schools that we envision, then—once they have accepted and are applying the principles outlined above as their minimum ground rules for operation—would legitimize a range of viable instructional options. Some may ask whether a Nazi school or an anti-white school for blacks could exist within the framework of a public system of choice. Obviously, *No. Our concept speaks to openness. It values diversity, it is democratic, it embraces human growth and development, and is unswerving in its recognition of individual worth.* Within these bounds, however, there is a full spectrum of alternative possibilities with new educational and learning forms. Schools could, for example, emphasize science or languages or the arts; they could be graded or ungraded, open or traditional, team-taught or self-contained, technical or non-technical; they could seek a multicultural approach or work to strengthen particular ethnic and group identities, examine the "third world" and be socially active; they could be housed in a "school" facility or use the community as a learning environment. Each, however, must meet the standard principles which are fundamental to a public school system of choice and must include *evaluation*.

Respecting the rights and responsibilities of others, for example, cannot work if the option being promulgated is based on an educational system which instills hate, or revenge, a system which advocates the imposition of one's own values on others. The Public Schools of Choice model can work only if the participants accept the ground rules of mutual respect and non-superimposition. While change is inherent in the plan, it is not based on a "push others" orientation. Rather, it is based on the conception of *attraction*, on the setting up of a flexible framework in which the participant is attracted to those alternatives that maximize human development for him.

Summarizing, then, under our ground rules for Public Schools of Choice, an acceptable alternative:

1. demonstrates adherence to a COMPREHENSIVE SET OF EDUCATIONAL OBJECTIVES—not particular ones. Proposals cannot, for example, emphasize only emotional growth at the expense of intellectual development. The converse is also true. Comprehensive educational objectives deal with work careers, citizenship, talent development, intellectual and emotional growth, problem solving, critical thinking, and the like.
2. does not SUBSTANTIALLY INCREASE THE PER STUDENT EXPENDITURE over that of established programs. To advance an idea which doubles or triples the budget will at best place the proposal in the category of ideal but not practical. An important factor for reformers to bear in mind is that the new arena will make wiser use of OLD money, not set up quests for add-on money.
3. does not ADVOCATE ANY FORM OF EXCLUSIVITY—racial, religious, or economic. Alternatives offered cannot deny equal access to any particular individual or group.

4. is not SUPERIMPOSED but a matter of choice for all participants—
teachers, parents and students.
5. is viewed as ANOTHER WAY of providing education alongside the
existing pattern, which continues to be legitimate. Alternatives are
different from special programs for dropouts, unwed mothers and
the like.
6. includes a plan for EVALUATION.

What constitutes a legitimate educational option under our
rules is a critical question.

Public schools have a responsibility to equip each learner with
the skills needed for economic, political, and social survival
in the stage of civilization in which we find ourselves; at the
same time, we must provide each learner with the tools needed
for improving, transforming, reconstructing the elements of the
environment generally recognized as inimical to the noblest
aspirations of the nation or as detrimental to the growth and
development of the individual.

Speaking practically, public schools must provide opportunities for each learner to discover his talents. Careers in an
advanced technological society are vastly different from those
required in, say, agrarian America in the nineteenth century. The
fact is that our public schools are necessarily manpower development centers, linking talent to economic careers. As such, public
schools encompass economic "livelihood" objectives as an important set of educational ends. If an educational option discounted
this set of objectives, it would be suspect as a legitimate alternative within the framework of public education.

This may be a roundabout way of saying again that public
schools must deal with a comprehensive set of educational objectives, and that the legitimacy of any option is determined by the
extent to which it adheres to the achievement of the *entire* set,
not just of *certain objectives*.

Public Schools of Choice can work only when students, parents, teachers and administrators all have equal access to educational options at both the conceptual and operational levels. But,

unless the parent or consumer is aware of the existence of new educational alternatives, he is left with only the ones with which he is at present familiar and is forced to "play" by the ground rules established by the existing system. The question which must be posed is, then: what mechanisms need be developed to bring relevant educational information to the public?

The administration of a school system might assume the leadership role by arranging informational meetings with the various groups involved. Such meetings could lead parent associations to hold meetings to explore a variety of educational options. Student groups at the elementary, junior high and high school levels, and teacher organizations could do the same thing. Depending on the response to these meetings, and after careful planning, trial programs could be launched, either in one school or in a cluster of schools. Under certain conditions, an entire school district could mount a special program.

While Public Schools of Choice works best when an entire school goes into the plan and provides many options for all students and teachers, it may be desirable to start by trying options not too dissimilar to the school's present operational style. Developing choices at the individual school level can, however, pose a number of problems. As the different segments of the public explore new options, a group might find itself in the "box" of scanning the almost endless laundry-list of reading materials, from ITA (Initial Teaching Alphabet) to *Dick and Jane*. This process is not necessarily bad, but it could leave the participants with a cold, one-sided view of the learning process. This is not to suggest that engaging in basic inquiry into different reading approaches is not beneficial, but only that initiation of such an inquiry at this level may ultimately discourage full participation because technical details may kill public interest.

If, on the other hand, a community undertook a conceptual examination of educational alternatives, the participants might indeed achieve a better background for decision-making. It is one thing to become knowledgeable about a concept or idea, and quite another to become familiar with the intricate details that go into making the idea work. While it is obvious that some knowledge of detail is necessary, one cannot expect students, parents, and citizens in general to be as well-informed about the subtleties of pedagogy as are professionals. To the professional educators—teachers and administrators—has been delegated the responsibility for the substance and techniques of education, but the consumer of a school system in our society must be responsible for determining the kind of education he wants. He must be provided, therefore, with the opportunity and conditions to enable him to perform this crucial policy role. Thus, a new standard of professional and lay participation could lead to more sensible educational conceptions, supported by both groups. Under a Public Schools of Choice model, different consumers would be matched with different professionals to develop a joint concept of quality education—again, so long as the ground rules are honored.

At the individual school level, therefore, if the major parties could study such concepts as Montessori Method, the Open Classroom, Behavior Modification, Multiculture, and so on, alternatives would probably move ahead rapidly. Or perhaps the educational concept to be studied might be the *approach:* "child-centered" versus "teacher-centered" or, the *structure,* e.g. graded or nongraded patterns?

One way to consider alternatives is to place them on a continuum according to how much freedom a student has to choose the elements of learning, i.e., how much freedom does the student have to choose the teacher, the content, the learning methodology, the time, the place. At one extreme, the learner selects what he shall learn, with whom, when, where and how. At this end of the continuum, the learner is most "free." At the other end, the learner has no choice of teacher, content, methodology, time, and place. At this end he is most dependent on the institutional procedures and requirements, i.e., the institution predetermines the conditions of learning for the student—who his teacher will be, how the teacher will teach, what the subject matter will be, how much time is spent on each subject, and when and where this learning takes place.

Between these extremes, there is a range of possibilities. The learner can be free to choose certain content areas, but not others which are required for everyone, e.g., reading, writing, arithmetic, physical education, health. He may have some freedom in how he wishes to approach these content areas, e.g., by reading a book, by viewing video tapes, by doing research, by listening to a lecture, by discussion with others, etc. He may have some freedom to choose the time and place to learn, e.g., he may enter into a contract with the teacher to accomplish a project by a certain time. He may decide to spend most of his school time for the first week on art, but spend considerable time after school hours on science. He may have access to resources in the community which he wishes to utilize—libraries, museums, television and radio stations, etc.

Consequently, using such an overlapping continuum, we can see that the free school alternative enables each learner to orchestrate his own education. The learner has complete freedom to select and use his own resources (of which the teacher is only one), whether these are in the school or not. He could choose not to study mathematics, science, spend most of his time pursuing his own interests, e.g., art, drama, etc.

There are obviously different types of free school alternatives —ranging from an Illich, Reimer model, which de-emphasizes schooling, to a Summerhill model, which uses school as a type of self-governing unit. Free school alternatives are the most difficult to legitimize under a public school framework at this time and will probably remain outside, as private alternative schools. They run counter to the emerging ground rules for alternative public schools.

The open phase of the continuum obviously overlaps with the free, but limits the range of choice the learner has. Thus, while a student can choose when and how he will learn science or math, and while no subject is forced, they are, nevertheless, still "required." They may take the form of "Learning Centers," i.e., areas that contain the resources for learning a particular subject area, but they are largely predetermined by the teacher, who helps guide the students in various content areas.

Such an educational continuum can be charted briefly as shown on page 50.

The British Infant, Montessori, and Schools Without Walls could be examples under the "open" category. Ungraded continuous progress, modular scheduling, behavior modification are possible alternatives under the "modified." Formally organized, age-graded schools, uniformly regimented academies tend to fall into "standard" options.

Once alternative education and the ground rules of the "choice" system are understood, an entire district may want to develop a framework of alternatives for its public schools. Here is a typical list from which parents, students, teachers and administrators can choose.

Alternative 1: The concept and programs of School No. 1 are traditional. It is graded and emphasizes the learning of basic skills— reading, writing, numbers, etc.—by cognition. The basic learning unit is the classroom, which functions with one or two teachers instructing and directing students at their various learning tasks. Students are encouraged to adjust to the school and its operational style, rather than vice versa. Students with recognized learning problems are referred to a variety of remedial and school-support programs. The educational and fiscal policy for this school is determined entirely by central board of education.

Alternative 2: The approach at School No. 2 is nontraditional and nongraded. In many ways it is very much like the British primary school and the Leicestershire system. There are lots of constructional and manipulative materials in each area where students work and learn. The teacher acts as a facilitator—one who assists and guides, rather than directs or instructs. Most student activity is in the form of different specialized learning projects carried on individually and

Alternatives on a Freedom-to-Prescription Continuum *

Free	Open	Modified	Standard
Learner-directed and -controlled. Learner has complete freedom to orchestrate his own education. Teacher is one resource.	Learner has considerable freedom to choose from a wide range of content areas considered relevant by teacher, parent, student. Resource centers in major skill areas made available to learner.	Prescribed content is made more flexible through individualization of instruction; school is ungraded; students learn same thing but at different rates. Using team teaching, teachers plan a differentiated approach to the same content. Teacher and programmed course of study are the major sources of student learning.	Learner adheres to institution requirements uniformly prescribed: what is to be taught—how, when, where, and with whom. Teacher is instructor-evaluator. Student passes or fails according to normative standards.
	Opening of school to the community and its resources.		
	Teacher is supportive guider.		
	Noncompetitive environment.		
		Teacher-student planning.	Competitive environments.
	No student failures. Curriculum is viewed as social system rather than as course of studies.		School is the major instructional setting.
Learner-centered.	Teacher-centered.	Subject-matter-centered.	Institution-centered.

in small groups, rather than in classes with all the students doing the same thing at the same time. Many of the learning experiences and activities take place outside the school building.

Alternative 3: School No. 3 emphasizes talent development and focuses on creative experiences, human services and concentration in a particular field, e.g. art, media, space, science, dramatics, music,

* Mario D. Fantini, "Alternatives Within Public Schools," Phi Delta Kappan, Special Issue on Alternative Schools, March 1973, pp. 447–8.

etc. The school defines its role as diagnostic and prescriptive. When the learner's talents are identified, the school orchestrates whatever experiences seem necessary to develop and enhance them. This school encourages many styles of learning and teaching. Students may achieve by demonstration and manipulation of real objects as well as by verbal, written or abstractive performances. All activity is specifically related to enhancing talent in relation to personal careers.

Alternative 4: School No. 4 is more oriented to technics than the others in the district. It utilizes computers to help diagnose individual needs and abilities. Computer-assisted instruction based on the diagnosis is subsequently provided both for individuals and groups. The library is stocked with tape-recording banks and "talking," "listening," and manipulative carrels that students can operate on their own. In addition, there are Nova-type video retrieval systems in which students and teachers can concentrate on specific problem areas. The school also has facilities for closed circuit television.

Alternative 5: School No. 5 is a total community school. It operates on a 12- to 14-hour basis at least six days a week throughout the year. It provides educational and other services for children of varying ages from the neighborhood, and evening classes and activities for adults. Services in such areas as health, legal aid and employment are available within the school facility. Paraprofessionals or community teachers are used in every phase of the regular school program. The school is governed by a community board which approves or hires two chief administrators: one who is in charge of the school, the other of all other activities in the building. The school functions as a center for the educational needs of all people in the neighborhood and community.

Alternative 6: School No. 6 is in fact a Montessori school. Students move at their own pace and are largely self-directed. The learning areas are rich in materials and specialized learning instruments from which the students can select as they wish. Although the teachers operate within a specific, defined methodology, they remain very much in the background, guiding students rather than directing them. Special emphasis is placed on the development of the five senses.

Alternative 7: Patterned after the Multi-Culture School in San Francisco, School No. 7 may have four or five ethnic groups equally represented in the student body. Students spend part of each day in racially heterogeneous learning groups. In another part of the day, all students and teachers of the same ethnic background meet together. In these classes, all learn their own culture, language, customs, history and heritage. Several times each week one ethnic group shares with the others some important educational event or aspect of its cultural heritage. This school views diversity as a value. Its curriculum combines the affective and cognitive domains and is humanistically oriented. Much time is spent on questions of identity, connectedness, power and powerlessness, and interpersonal relationships. The school is run by a policy board made up of equal numbers of parents and teachers, and is only tangentially responsible to a central board of education.

Alternative 8: School No. 8 is a Performance Contract School. The educational consumer may want to sub-contract with an educational firm to operate one of its public schools. In Gary, Indiana, Behavioral Research Laboratories operated the Banneker Elementary School. Under a contract with the public schools, the contract contained a money-back guarantee that the children in the school would achieve a certain set of educational objectives, i.e. reading at grade level. The Banneker program made wide use of individualized reading materials developed by the company.

In an actual case, Quincy Senior High II in Quincy, Illinois, established seven alternatives in a school-within-a-school program. Called Education by Choice, this approach to options proceeded after a comprehensive planning effort involving teachers, students and parents.

The result of this planning process was the development of seven educational alternatives. These alternatives are briefly described as follows:

1. An option which presents a learning environment that is primarily teacher directed. (Standard)
2. An option which presents a learning environment that receives direction from both teacher and student, but for the most part would be teacher directed. (Flexible)
3. An option which presents a learning environment where students and teachers together plan the experiences for the participants. (Individualized)
4. An option which presents a learning environment where the primary focus is consideration of the various areas of learning in relation to the arts. (Fine Arts)

5. An option which presents a learning environment where the primary focus is centered around career orientation and preparation. (Career)
6. An option which presents a learning environment for special education students. (Special Education)
7. An option which presents a learning environment for dropout-prone students. (Work Study)

Intensive sessions were held with all the teachers of this eleventh-and-twelfth-grade high school. In March 1973, each teacher was given a first and second choice from among the seven options.

This was followed by assemblies for the 1,500 students describing the program, printed information outlining the plan in greater detail, and finally an opportunity for each student to make his first and second choices. The students signed for their choices during a special time period in which tables were set up for each of the seven options. Teachers manned each table.

Also, a series of parent meetings were held on the Education by Choice plan. Over five hundred parents attended these sessions.

Finally each teacher, student and parent made a choice. Each student made a choice alone and with his parents. The breakdown, as reported by Rick Haugh, Project Coordinator for Education by Choice, is as follows: *

Alternative	Teacher Choice	Student and Parent Choice
Standard	13	276
Flexible	14	345
Individualized	12	306
Fine Arts	9	130
Career	12	184
Special Education	3	45
Work Study	7	115

* Reported in a telephone conversation, March 20, 1973.

Mr. Haugh explained that there were few problems; almost all received his or her first choice.

The Quincy case demonstrates that teachers have different preferences based on their own teaching style. Also, if given a choice from among a number of alternatives, most teachers will not choose the same option. The same seems true for students and parents.

Should there have been a greater demand for one or two of the alternatives, then an in-service program could be mounted to help teachers retool and prepare for them. It is well to remember that in this case, as in most efforts at developing alternative education, teachers are asked to make a choice based on their existing style of teaching. Many teachers learned this style naturally. However, it is possible that many teachers could develop a number of approaches if the preparatory or staff development program were designed to help differentiate teaching styles.

This is another way of stating that alternatives help give new direction to in-service education of teachers. Certainly, if some options are in greater demand than others, then certain teachers, perhaps those who express the desire, can be helped to staff them. After all, if there were no options, the teacher would still require in-service education.

The Public Schools of Choice system would be a *renewal* system, that is, the options under a broad public framework would be judged by results. As the results associated with quality education were more realized in one model than in another, the attractiveness of the successful would grow. The options that are more successful will most likely be in more demand, thus triggering a self-renewing process.

III / MATCHING TEACHING-LEARNING STYLES

As we can sense, alternate forms of education are based on different styles of teaching and learning. These are now largely hidden by the uniform framework of our public schools. They exist on a random basis. Differences among schools are at this moment more a matter of social class than of program. Differences among teachers are minimized.

At present, options are available, but primarily to the upper-middle class in the form of private schools. For the masses, the uniform public schools have been the only option. Moreover, public school systems, in order to be equitable to the public, have tried to render all public schools identical. By manipulating all learners toward the same model, the school, instead of equalizing educational opportunities, has produced the exact opposite for many students and teachers.

Once teachers are certified, they are perceived as being "the same." Teachers, all different people with different styles of teaching, find it natural to close the doors of their classrooms and try to deal with twenty-five to thirty-five learners as a block. They try to deal with these learners by imposing one style of teaching on the group. There are many children who respond positively to this style, and just as many who do not. Those who do not are often called "slow," "deprived," even "retarded." By classifying the children, the teacher is also developing an institutionalized way of thinking about them, and constructing a web of self-fulfilling prophecies: what the teacher expects is usually what she gets.

In my own case, when I began as a teacher, I literally walked into the classroom and expected every child to adjust to me. It was difficult for me to realize that my style of teaching simply did not, indeed, could not, make contact with all the learners. I found it comfortable to label the children who were not adjusting "slow," and to recommend placing them in special classes for "slow learners."

It did not then occur to me that certain children were not responding to me because for them there was something wrong with *my* teaching style—with *my* approach—not with the student's style of learning. The fact was that the very children who did not respond to my style were responding to the English teacher across the hall from me, who had a different approach. In this case the difference in student response was not due to the difference in course content but in teacher style. There was simply no productive match of teaching and learning styles. Thus, the school, by viewing all teachers as being alike and by requiring students to be assigned to teachers either randomly or by ability-grouping (i.e., by how well the student was doing academically), was actually perpetuating unequal education.

If one were to walk into any public school, he would soon learn that teachers possess different personalities and teaching styles. This notion of style, while difficult to define, can be easily spotted. We can spot style in actors, singers, political figures, poets, etc. Why not in teachers?

Many teachers have similar teaching styles. These similar styles, if grouped together, generate similar educational environments. Teachers, individually or in groups, produce different kinds of classroom environments, different types of classroom social structure. Some emphasize a certain approach to learning which is markedly different from that of other groups of teachers with other styles of teaching. We have teacher styles generating "informal" classrooms, "schools without walls," "formal" classrooms, etc. Behind each alternative is a teacher or group of teachers with the same basic style. The liberation of the teacher's style through the sanctioning of educational alternatives may make more visible the existence of legitimate differences among teachers, differences which can help individualize learning, increase educational productivity, and enhance professional satisfaction.

Note the difference between two elementary school teachers in the same school.

. . . you might examine a classroom and see the teacher in the front of the room talking to the class. The class might be listening and taking notes; if an assignment is being made, the students might ask questions. Soon the class is over and a new class comes in. The teacher again asks for the homework from the previous day, goes on to some new work, dictates some important facts, asks a few questions on the work which should have been prepared for the day, makes an assignment for the following day, and answers some last-minute questions. Then a new group comes in and the pattern is repeated.

You might then examine another room where the teacher is, at first, hard to find. She is in the background, but the students are moving around freely. Various projects are being undertaken by small groups of students, while other students are working alone. There does not seem to be a routinized approach.*

* Mario D. Fantini, "Open vs. Closed Classrooms," in *Clearing House,* Vol. 37, No. 2, October 1962.

Certain educators might consider the first classroom described above as being "teacher-directed," and the second classroom as being more "student-directed." Other schoolmen might prefer the term "subject-matter centered" to describe the first teacher and "learner-centered" to describe the second. These and other phrases are attempts to capture the main thrust of the teacher's approach in the classroom.

One way to get a handle on the matter of individual teaching style—or student learning style—is to consider the method used for teaching and learning. Classically, methods can be viewed as being either more *inductive* or more *deductive*. In the inductive approach, one proceeds from the specific to the abstract, from particular information to some generalization. For instance, a child may have several objects which he throws into the air. Each drops. After several trials, he may conclude that everything that goes up must come down. Once he has formed such a generalization, he can apply it to other situations.

The important point here is that the learner discovered the broad principle for himself.

In a deductive approach, the person may begin with the generalization such as everything that goes up must come down. He then proceeds to test the generalization by throwing several objects into the air, etc.

With the deductive approach, the underlying principle is learned and then applied to different situations.

Harvard psychologist Jerome Bruner relates an incident derived from one of his observations of a classroom situation, which was indicative of an inductive teaching method. The case in point was a class in which the teacher presented geography, not as a set of knowns, but as a set of unknowns. The class was presented with maps showing only such details as the tracings of rivers and lakes, and, perhaps, some natural resources. The students were asked as a first exercise to show where they felt the principal cities, the railroads, and the main highways would be located. No books or maps were permitted. At the completion of this exercise, a class discussion followed in which various children, by citing general principles, attempted to justify the positions they had taken in allocating certain spots on the maps for the major cities, railroads and the like. As a result, a very stimulating discussion ensued. After close to an hour, and after much pleading by the children, the class finally did roll down the detailed map and compared what they had developed on their own maps with what was actually evidenced by the wall map. Many students responded enthusiastically, with such impromptu actions as shouting for joy when a major city like Chicago had been spotted successfully. Those who did not duplicate the wall map responded with such rationalizations as: "just because Chicago is there, it doesn't mean that that is where it should be—the rivers are not situated properly."

The same lesson treated deductively may have begun with the teacher, textbook or film giving the student the generalization that major cities are located on major navigational waterways. The student would have to master the generalization and then demonstrate his understanding by naming a number of cities that support the generalization.

Both approaches are valid. No teaching is all inductive or all deductive. In fact, when these approaches are translated into the school and classroom setting, they could have different meanings.

The deductive approach has come to mean a teacher or school-controlled structure in which known knowledge in various disciplines is systematically covered. This structure has come to mean studying and mastering the known, where knowledge is more prescribed by the teacher.

Inductive teaching has come to mean generating a structure in which problems are solved by doing, by engaging in hands-on activities that lead to solutions—of finding out about the unknown—of having the student attempt to give order to what may appear to be disorder.

Certain inductive approaches emphasize problem-solving. Real problems become the focus for interdisciplinary learning. A class is confronted with a problem. In the process of trying to resolve the problem, the children can use their English studies, math, social studies, science, arts and crafts, music, and the like. Here is how one teacher describes a problem-solving experience:

A class trip to a suburban farm school resulted in the presentation of a pet rabbit to the class. What to do with the pet became the central problem. The class discussed ways of providing care and shelter for their new addition, and soon the children were eagerly bringing in wood for a cage. Their enthusiasm spread to the community and resulted in the presentation of other pets. Soon the rabbit had as neighbors a rooster, a turtle, albino rats, and guinea pigs.

New problems arose. The children had enough pets to fill a house. And a house for the pets is exactly what the class undertook to build in the classroom. Planning, grouping, and creating went along with the lively business of building. Excited by the possibilities, the children came up with the idea of using electricity in the house and making an electrical robot to greet visitors who might want to see the project.

The classroom was filled with children's work. Drawings of electrical circuits were mounted on the bulletin board. Posters on the care and feeding of pets went up. Exhibits of animals the children had made out of clay and papier-mâché brightened the room.

The classroom became the children's workshop. Not to be an active participant was considered severe punishment.

Academic skills found new meaning when they were used with the rich and varied activities that grew out of the program. The children weighed pets, marked prices, and wrestled with word problems. They wrote stories about their work and their pets, and the stories were bound together to make a science reader that was their own work. They composed songs about animals, set up a pet library, and staged dramatic productions on various phases of pet care. The children learned by experience that it was necessary to master certain skills in reading, writing, spelling, and arithmetic.

The finished, concrete projects—the animal house, the cages, the electrical circuits, the robot, the charts, the posters—all were end products of processes that led to real learning for these children.

The boys and girls in this classroom became the center of interest in both the school and the community, and the attention was a tonic for their sense of worth and belonging.

The children lived in harmony with one another, for they were doing work they wanted to do, and their energy was channeled toward constructive ends. It was expressed not in behavior problems but in cooperation with others to achieve a common purpose.

They learned through experiences that involved planning, self-direction, discovery, exploration, and thinking. Learning was individualized to the extent that children defined their goals as a group and proceeded toward their goals independently, as individuals, in an atmosphere of freedom and acceptance.

What was the teacher's role throughout this program? He was a catalyst, remaining in the background, guiding the children through the excitement of learning, letting his teaching shine through the behavior of the pupils.*

With inductive methods, "facts" are not taken for granted. The answers are not presented beforehand, but emerge through the process of inquiry. In this process, the learner starts with certain data and a problem and he tries to hypothesize conclusions and check them in a search for solutions. This is the inductive method of teaching. Conversely, the deductive method would give the learner the "truth" first, and follow that application of the "truth" to other problems and situations.

For instance, a teacher may have the children examine a colorless liquid and pose the problem "What is it?" The children may infer an answer: water, mineral oil, alcohol, etc. The children may be asked how they would proceed to find out which one.

A deductive lesson may proceed by giving the learner the

* Mario D. Fantini, "Let's Make Learning Exciting for Slow Learners, Too," in *The Elementary School Journal*, October 1960, pp. 12–13.

name of the liquid in question, its composition, etc. This could be repeated for other liquids. The learner may be asked to test his knowledge of liquids by being able to identify them in a test situation; e.g., a series of bottles, each containing a liquid, is presented, and the learner, by applying his knowledge of the characteristics of each liquid, would proceed to identify each.

Another example of inductive teaching concerns a social studies lesson on government. In order to establish a particular perspective, this case description will be presented more fully than the others I have cited.

Teacher A, inductively oriented, began with a set of questions: "Why do we need organization?" "Why are we arranged this way in the class?" "Why are you in school at all?" "Who made the law saying you must go to school?" "Why do we make laws?" Teacher A continued, "Suppose I were not here in the classroom; what would you do?" This line of questioning continued. The children's books did not contain answers to these questions, so the children were left on their own to think through the solutions. This was a new group for Teacher A. For many students, this was their first encounter with this method. The class discussion which followed took the entire period. At the end of the discussion, certain students came out with this broad concept: "Organization is necessary *if anything productive* is to be achieved. Without organization, there would be chaos."

The following day, the teacher greeted the group with: "All right, we arrived at a broad concept yesterday." She had used the word *concept* right after the students had arrived at their conclusion, and the term now seemed to make more sense to the students, who understood the "broad concept" they had worked out.

"Today," the teacher continued, "let us search for answers to this problem: Suppose there is just this school, and no one else near us. Suppose further that here in this room we have a way of producing food, and, suppose, moreover, that other rooms have other products or talents to offer. How will we all live? How are we to supply our needs?" This problem triggered a discussion of what our basic needs are.

The teacher continued to ask questions: "What are the alternatives open to us in attempting to supply our needs? Is what we do motivated by our desire to satisfy our needs? Which of the alternatives you have suggested is the best way?" The students discussed certain ideas, until, finally, they reached the conclusion that there were, indeed, different ways of organizing themselves into a society. In their own words the students categorized organization in types corresponding to the terms *dictatorial, communistic, democratic,* and *anarchistic.*

The next assignment was for each person to think about how he himself would like to have society organized. The students gave labels to each method of organization which they had identified. They gave such names as *Zenda, Aban, Redz,* and *Delta* to their ideas. The teacher continued to guide them indirectly. "All right," she said, "how would you like to live under a Zenda organization?" For a whole week the class had an opportunity to live under a kind of Zenda (dictatorship). The second week they tried Aban (communism), and the week after they tried Redz (anarchy). Finally, the last week, they tried Delta (democracy). After the exercise was over, the teacher provided opportunities for the children to read about communism, democracy, anarchy, and dictatorship, in an attempt to square off their own opinions with those of experts. With democracy, the teacher added a further dimension by having them compare their own concept of democratic organization, with the ideas expressed by the founding fathers of this nation. The investigation led the students to the realization that our democracy had deviated from some of its original ideals. Finally, they sought a clearer definition of their role as American citizens in bringing about the changes needed for what they now saw as truly democratic functioning.

Teacher B, more prescriptive in her teaching, approached the same problem of ways in which people organize, by asking the class the same question as Teacher A: "Why do we need organization?" A class discussion followed, and then an assignment. "Chapter Two of our text deals with the different forms of government. You read it tonight for homework. Chapter Two gives us clear definitions for communism, dictatorship, socialism, and so on . . ." The next day, Teacher B asked the class, "What is a dictatorship?" A student answered, "One-man rule!" The teacher reinforced the answer by saying, "This is what we want to remember about dictatorship, and *this* is what we want to remember about fascism." A chalkboard was used to outline the major points of the lesson.

The teacher might have asked for specific characteristics from the class and listed these on the board. For instance:

1. One man rule
2. The government controls the resources of the state
3. Freedom of speech and of the press are restricted, etc.

The outline on the chalkboard was entered in the students' notebooks to be reviewed by them at such a time as the teacher determined that a test was needed. At test time, the student, having studied his text and his notes, proceeded to answer questions posed by the teacher. A passing grade indicated that the students had satisfactorily learned *what the book had said* about the forms of government.

A second example involved a science lesson with fifth graders on "the earth." In this case, the inductively minded teacher opened the inquiry with the question "How do you think the earth was formed?" A discussion followed, in which certain factors were identified, and others isolated. Soon, good guesses were forthcoming. These the teacher labeled "theories." After several promising "theories" had been recorded, an assignment was made to check these class theories with those recorded in the science book, and to note similarities and differences. The children were also asked to explain why they thought the differences existed.

This same lesson was approached by a teacher with deductive tendencies with the teacher writing the subject of the lesson on the chalkboard, "How the Earth Began."

"Today," the teacher said, "we will learn how the earth that we live on began. To start us off, we are going to see a movie on the earth. After the movie, we will have a discussion."

A film on the earth was shown, which described in cartoon fashion how some scientists think the earth and the universe began.

After the film, the teacher asked the class, "What is the "Big Bang" Theory?" Several children gave answers. "For tomorrow, I want you to read Chapter Two of your science book. This chapter is called The Earth. Please read the chapter carefully and be able to answer the questions at the end of the chapter."

The reason the examples of inductive teaching appear longer is that this approach emphasizes *process* and is more time-consuming. The deductive approach also emphasizes process, but tends to be more prescriptive and less time-consuming because the major idea is often presented first.

In these examples, both versions of the inductive and deductive approaches obviously made contact with many youngsters. It is possible that these learners preferred to approach learning in this way. However, there were students in both classes who seemed lost, frustrated and unhappy with the approaches. Some students in the "inductive" class would have preferred a more deductively oriented teacher. They were more at home—learned more—with a teacher who was more directive, who systematically and logically proceeded to cover the subject matter. Most of us in our childhood were exposed to such directive teachers. Somehow, this seems more normal to us. Teachers are supposed to know their subject. Many students who are with inductive teachers complain that they are not learning anything when they are on their own, but only when the teacher is directive, i.e. actually "teaches" in front of the class.

Often in my travels through schools, I note the problems arising from a mismatch of teaching-learning styles. For example, in one classroom, the teacher was using a non-directive, inductive approach, trying to elicit a response by asking questions, without himself giving the answers. About half the class participated, i.e., interacted with the teacher. When we stopped the class to analyze the situation with the students, the nonparticipating students began to voice their discontent with the teacher's approach. "I came here to listen and to learn something from someone who is an expert—instead, I have to sit here listening to a discussion."

When the entire class was asked to show by raising their hands how many preferred the approach in which the teacher was non-directive, about half the students did so; the other half preferred a type of structure in which the teacher presented his or her knowledge directly to the class, through lectures, assignments and tests.

In some classrooms in which there is a mismatch of teaching and learning styles, the climate for everyone suffers. That is to say, those who are "turned off" by the style become bored and turn their energies to activities which are disruptive. Some of these mismatched students are then labeled "disruptive" or "slow." But the problem may not be so much with lack of ability as a lack of compatibility between the teaching and the learning styles. Teaching style does generate a certain type of social system in the classroom. Some classrooms are informal, with students talking to one another and moving about, while other classrooms are quiet and routinized. Again, certain students may be comfortable with each situation. Personality is also an element of style. Some learners prefer teachers who are strong, dramatic or extroverted; others prefer a more quiet, subdued teacher. Some teachers are friendly; others are more detached. It is possible to have a quiet, detached, inductively oriented teacher—and a dramatic, deductively disposed teacher, and vice-versa. Some teachers deal with control or discipline by "laying down the law" and holding everyone to obey the rules or face strict punishment. Other teachers prefer to develop class rules in cooperation with students. When class laws are broken, some teachers punish the students themselves; others rely on the school administration. Still other teachers prefer that students assist in the enforcement of discipline. Some teachers prefer "to talk things out" with individual students. Other teachers "draw the line" and will not consider involving themselves personally in student problems.

All of us could go on mentioning teachers we have had who impressed us for one reason or another. The point here is that since both students and teachers are of many sorts, it improves learning to seek a more harmonious match between them. This is one of the many ways of individualizing instruction, and that is one of the cardinal principles of education.

Another way to consider achieving a more fruitful match of teaching-learning styles is suggested by David E. Hunt of the Ontario Institute for Studies in Education. According to Hunt, et al, learners develop conceptually through various stages. Conceptual levels (CL) refers to the degree of conceptual complexity or interpersonal maturity of the learner. The child passes through a sequence of stages proceeding from an immature, unsocialized Stage A to a dependent, conforming Stage B, to an independent self-reliant Stage C.

Using the conceptual-levels model, Hunt and his colleagues

worked in two schools, one elementary, one junior high. Students were grouped according to conceptual stage (learning style) and teachers were matched with each group by the methods and procedures used (teaching style).
Hunt reports the following matches:

Group	Characteristics	Methods and Procedures *
Classroom A (Very low CL)	"Short attention span." "Like to be active; there is constant movement." "A lot of physical and verbal fights." "Do not know how to function in group situations or discussions." "Incapable of thinking through a problem; will guess and let it go at that." "Try the rules often." "Work only because the teacher says so, and look to peers for approval."	"Specific step-by-step instructions." "Make goals and deadlines short and definite." "Give immediate feedback on each step." "Praise often." "Use pictures and things they can see and touch." "Assign definite seats." "Get them to work immediately and change pace often." "Because of inability to discuss, do more seat work."
Classroom B (Low CL)	"Oriented to the role of a 'good student,' one who got the right answers, had neat work and good work habits." "Seek teacher approval." "Want to work alone at their own desks." "Incapable of adjusting to a different teacher." "Upset by visitors or alterations of the schedule." "Do not express personal options." "Are confused by choices." "Want to be told and have the teacher constantly present."	"Have them initially in rows and gradually get them working in pairs, then in small groups." "Use creative drama to encourage spontaneity, self-awareness and cooperation." "Provide non-threatening situations where they have to risk an opinion." "Provide a lot of praise and success oriented situations."

* David E. Hunt, JoAnn Greenwood, Ronald Brill. "From Psychological Theory to Educational Practice: Implementation of a Matching Model." Paper presented at a symposium, "Models of Teaching and Learning," American Educational Research Association Meeting, Chicago, Illinois, April 7, 1972, pp. 10–11.

Group	Characteristics	Methods and Procedures
Classroom D/E (High CL)	"Like to discuss and argue." "Everybody wants to talk at once and nobody listens." "Will question and volunteer additional information." "Want to solve things themselves." "Go off on sidetracks." "Don't require teacher rewards." "Are imaginative." "Are not afraid of making mistakes." "Are enthusiastic and eager to go off on things on their own." "See alternatives." "Are averse to detail and can not tolerate going step-by-step." "Can stay at one thing for a long time."	"Don't require definite seating plan." "Give them many topics from which to choose." "Set weekly requirements and students make up their own timetable." "Encourage them to use each other as resources." "Have to be trained to listen to instructions as they tend to go off on their own."

In introducing their ideas to parents, students and teachers, Hunt and his associates pass out the following description which also supports the need to find better ways of matching teaching-learning styles:

Learning Styles and Teaching Methods

Students differ in how they learn, or in their *learning styles*. For example, some learn better by listening to the teacher, some by discussions, and others by working on their own. To say that students differ in their learning styles does not mean that a student needs only one approach exclusively, but that, generally speaking, he has one way of learning which for him is better than others.

Similarly, teachers use a variety of approaches, or *teaching methods*. For example, they may lecture, they may discuss, or they may let the student discover for himself. That is not to say that lecture, discussion, and independent study are the only methods, but they illustrate the variety in ways of teaching. No teacher uses one method exclusively, but he tries to use the method most likely to work with a specific class.

Grouping students by learning style enables the teacher to use that teaching method most likely to work for the majority of students in that class. To say that the teacher will try to match the teaching methods to the class learning style does not mean that only one approach is used. For example, a teacher working with a class whose predominant learning style is for independent learning will not always assign them to work on their own. The teacher will use a variety of approaches with each class, and will ask students in each class to give their opinions and ideas about teaching methods throughout the year. Therefore, finding the learning style of the class gives the teacher some general idea about what teaching method is likely to work best.

Regardless of the class learning style, all classes will learn the same material. It is the *way they learn* which will differ, not what or how much they learn. Grouping by learning style is simply a procedure to make it more likely that the teacher can meet the needs of the students.*

Still another way to categorize different teaching styles is to place the style of each teacher on a scale-continuum ranging from "formal" to "informal." Some of the characteristics which differentiate the two extremes of the scale are listed here:

Open	*Traditional*
Informal environment and human interaction	Formal environment and human interaction
Activity duration is child controlled	Activity time-scheduled by teacher
Teacher structures environment and process	Teacher structures curriculum
Teacher provides guidance, facilitates learning	Teacher provides the sources of learning
Furniture type and arrangement are based on the child's workshop pattern	Furniture type and arrangement follow a standard pattern
Individual or small group activity predominates	Whole-class oriented activity predominates
Children and visitors integrated	Children and visitors segregated
Teacher-pupil interaction individualistic	Teacher dominant, child subordinate
Curriculum is planned to meet children's interests	Curriculum is planned to cover teacher's lesson plan
Emphasis on abundance of concrete materials to manipulate	Dominance of textbook

* Hunt, *op. cit.*, p. 24.

Open	Traditional
Teacher non-authoritarian; acts as facilitator	Teacher controls, is disciplinarian
No difference between work and play	Dichotomized work and play
Learning by discovery	Learning by being taught
Grouping for several ages	Grouping for single age
Teacher and children determine pattern for the day	Teacher decides who does what and when
Child's education the child's responsibility	Child's education the teacher's responsibility
Emphasis on affective emotional as well as cognitive intellectual skills	Emphasis on intellectual development only
Evaluation as diagnosis	Evaluation as classification

Herb Kohl's book *The Open Classroom* appeals to those teachers whose teaching styles generate open educational environments. Similarly, when Charles Silberman in his *Crisis in the Classroom* points to the open British Infant School as a promising reform, he is making a plea to legitimize a freer educational environment in our schools.

Under our present structure teachers must now almost "sneak" the freer teaching style into the classroom. Many teaching styles are restricted by the uniform ground rules of the public itself. A teacher whose style inclines toward open education finds that, unless his approach to education is recognized as legitimate and considered *bona fide* by other teachers, administrators, and parents, he has to camouflage his preference in public and try to exercise his individual method only in the privacy of his classroom.

But through Public Schools of Choice we have an opportunity to encourage teachers to free their teaching styles. *Most important, such a new structure also supports teachers whose style is standard. While some learners are attracted to open education, others—indeed, most—would continue to profit from the standard. Both styles are needed.* It would be an error to favor only those whose teaching styles are "open," or to assume that all learners would learn better from open education. This simply is not the case, and assuming that it is would only serve to repeat past errors. We are not here advocating the substitution of one orthodoxy for another. Rather, we are encouraging educational pluralism.

A letter from a parent whose child is in a school in which both open and standard education are offered makes the point clear:

. . . My topic for this issue of the Newsletter is the open classroom. As you are aware, the Campus School has been involved in an experiment with the open classroom approach in the lower grades (as has been the Duzine School). Simply defined, it is an approach to teaching in which students are at certain times of the school day free to explore activities and learning from a variety of opportunities within the classroom. During these times, some children may decide to paint, some to dance, some to read, and others to work with building materials. The activities are chosen by the student according to his interests, not dictated by a set of lessons scheduled by the teacher. The classroom environment is thus full of materials and alternative opportunities, and not dominated by neat rows of desks and chairs. The teacher—and where practical, a team of teachers and teacher aides—moves about the classroom from group to group and individual to individual offering guidance and direction.

This approach to learning should not be labeled necessarily as a "permissive" approach, in the usual way that that term is used. The teacher is intimately involved in directing, guiding, cajoling, disciplining, and providing instruction. This open classroom approach merely opens up alternative activities and learning situations for the students.

In my opinion, and those of many others, not all children flourish in this type of environment. Some require more traditional, structured situations, in which the teacher narrows the range of activities and freedoms of expression for the child. The open classroom approach is not *the* answer to our educational problems. But, for some children, this opening up of the classroom provides opportunities for the gifted, creative child to explore learning activities more at his own pace, not held back by the average children. And it can provide opportunities for the slower learning child to spend extra time (under the guidance of the sensitive teacher aware of those deficiencies) in areas of learning where he needs it.

I am afraid that many parents are awaiting the results of evaluation of the open classroom approach in order to condemn it to a burial place, or, for others, to place it at the center of our educational programs and to drop the more traditional approaches. This would be a disastrous development. Evaluation of the ways that this new approach is working, or not working, are very needed. But, I have the feeling that the final verdict will be mixed—some parents and educators feeling vindicated in their enthusiasm for it, and others pointing to their suspicions earlier with glee. . . .*

The Education by Choice Model in the Quincy Public Schools shows the different learning environments that will be available to both students and teachers in their program. As we can see, the "structured," "modified," and "informal" teaching-learning styles will be served:

T = teacher
S = student

1. This option could provide a learning environment which is primarily teacher-controlled. A school incorporating some of the ideas of the Classic School or the Structured School with Student Input could create this environment.

2. This option could provide a learning environment which would receive direction from both teacher and student, but for the most part would be teacher-controlled. A school incorporating some of the ideas of the Modular School or the Individualized Instruction School might create this environment.

3. This option could provide a learning environment where teachers and students together would plan the learning experiences. A school incorporating the ideas of Project To Individualize Education or the Open School could create this environment.†

* Letter cited in *The Educational Horizon*, by David W. McDowell, Campus School PTA Second Vice President, and Assistant Professor, Department of Educational Studies, State University College, New Paltz, New York.

† Education by Choice Project, Quincy Public Schools, Title III, ESEA, Illinois. Grant No. 312–1–72.

Alternative schools, then, tend to attract teachers with similar teaching styles who together orchestrate a particular kind of learning environment. Students who feel that a particular environment best fits their style of learning will tend to choose it.

CAN PARENTS AND STUDENTS CHOOSE THE RIGHT STYLE?

One of the first questions raised about the Public Schools of Choice plan concerns the ability of the parents and students to make wise decisions. "What do parents know about which educational option or style is best for their children?" There are several ways in which a parent may approach this matter. He may want more information on the options themselves. If the student is old enough, the parent may depend a good deal on the opinion of the child himself. The parent may feel unprepared to make a choice, and request that the school use its own professional judgment in placing the child. The parent here makes a decision even when he *delegates* this responsibility to the school, e.g., to a principal, a teacher or a psychological counselor.

Still, most parents and professional educators alike ask: "Can children choose the right option? Are they capable of making such an important choice?" While those who raise such queries can accept more readily the notion of older students (in secondary schools) making such decisions, they become more skeptical with the younger children.

Usually young children can make decisions, not by saying "I prefer option A over B," but by how they relate to each environment. That is to say, a seven-year-old child does not fill out a form indicating his preference. Usually a conference between parents and school staff accomplishes this. However, the child makes the final decision by how well he accepts the option. If the child makes a happy adjustment, then he has made a decision. If he complains, then he is raising questions and has not made a decision.

Since each option is legitimate, i.e., as *bona fide* as any other, then the child can go from one to another alternative until he or she finds one that is compatible.

With older children it is possible for differences to develop among teachers, parents and students concerning the "right" alternative. For instance, a parent may prefer a standard option and the student a school without walls. In such cases, the teacher and other school officials try to provide as much information as possible about the alternative to both parent and student. If asked, the professional can present his opinion. But in the last analysis, it is a family matter. The decision is in their hands.

Parent and student decision-making is basic to a public school operation. In one sense, it is like a physician recommending an operation to his patient. Whether or not to operate is a decision for the patient as citizen—not for the doctor. The doctor can recommend, even urge, but the final decision rests with the patient. Similarly, in public schools, the professional educator may recommend, or urge—but the ultimate decision must come from the parent. It is to be hoped that the decision will usually be a cooperative effort in which the parent, student and professional adviser are agreed. At times, of course, such a decision may be a family affair—one where parents and child think through the situation together. But, in cases where there is disagreement, the final decision must be parental. In my experience, however, cases of extreme disagreement are few in number. It is far more likely that parents will delegate their responsibility to the professional educator.

Certainly, as we have emphasized, an important component of a Public Schools of Choice plan is parent and student education on the range of educational alternatives. Providing this basic information insures that those making the decisions have been prepared to make wise choices. For the past several years the

United Bronx Parents, Inc., in New York City have developed an ongoing parent and community education program related to their schools. Carefully prepared handbooks with pictures that help make salient points are provided. Basic questions are raised in these handbooks, and guidelines are offered for working out individual answers. Handbooks have been prepared with such titles as *How to Choose the Right School for Your Child: A Handbook for Voucher School Parents*, and *How Good Is Your Child's School?*

In the Voucher Handbook, for instance, parents are asked, "What type of school is right for your youngster?" The narrative goes on to explain—"All schools are not alike. Just as people wear different styles of clothing, so schools offer different styles of education."

Two pictures illustrating the difference between a traditional, formal school and an open, informal school are presented, together with the following description of each:

Traditional, Formal Schools

Parents remember this kind of school from their own childhood. The teacher is in charge of the class. The students raise their hands before speaking. Classes are organized into grades. A definite curriculum must be completed before a student is promoted. Tests and marks are frequently given. Some people call this the "no-nonsense" type of school.

Open, Informal Schools

Here the curriculum grows out of the pupil's own interest and curiosity. Students don't sit at desks all the time, but are free to walk around and help each other. Each child is encouraged to learn at his own pace and develop his own projects and tests. Some people call this the "child-centered" school.*

* *How to Choose the Right School for Your Child: A Handbook for Voucher School Parents*, United Bronx Parents, Inc., New York, N.Y.

Further, by actually giving the individual learner (and parent) the right to choose the educational alternative that he feels is best suited for him, we are providing him with a sense of control over his own destiny.

Psychologists are now revealing that "fate control"—the ability of an individual to sense control over his destiny—is basic to all motivation and achievement. In a major survey of American schools called *Equality of Educational Opportunities*, undertaken by the United States Office of Education, the chief investigator, James Coleman, offered the following conclusion:

. . . the extent to which an individual feels that he has some control over his destiny appears to have a stronger relationship to achievements than do all the "school" factors together.

Moreover, if a student selects an educational option which satisfies his own style, he is more likely to be interested in schooling. If a learner succeeds in an educational environment he himself has chosen, his own sense of self-worth will certainly be enhanced. These factors are important to maximum learning. Again, Coleman makes the point from his study:

. . . of all the variables measured in the survey, the attitudes of student interest in school, self-concept, and sense of environmental control show the greatest relation to achievement.

Developing learning alternatives also permits a *humanizing* of our public schools and the educational process. We all know how it feels to be lost in a large, mass-production type of educational institution and know the shortcomings of that type of school. When public elementary and secondary schools have from 500 to 5000 students, it is difficult—given the present structure—to get close to each learner—to know him as a person —to individualize according to his style, etc. Instead, schools, in the name of efficiency, become like factories, processing students in the same way that an automobile is processed. Anonymity and detachment become pervasive for students, staff and community.

Yet, most parents, teachers and school administrators long for a more intimate, more manageable grouping to insure the human dimension—to develop a sense of belonging, to individualize. Public Schools of Choice, because it permits small sub-units to develop, gets at the heart of the dehumanizing "mass production" problem. For example, "mini" schools of seventy-five to a hundred and fifty students can be formed in which small groups of learners are matched with teams of teachers. Children in such closely knit units are not "lost in the crowd." They become part of a "family" grouping. The size of the unit obviously helps teachers know each child, and *vice versa*.

When smallness of size of the group is coupled with choice of educational environment for child, parent and staff, a giant step toward humanistic education has been taken.

ALTERNATIVE STYLES AND VALUES

While I have gone to some length in advocating an increase in the number of educational styles and options, the reader should keep in mind that different alternatives may generate different *values*. An educational environment is a context in which human values are learned. The structure, the interaction patterns, the very learning process, made salient by the particular alternative offered, emphasize certain values. For example, a competitive educational structure in which children vie with other children for grades is likely to develop in learners different values from those developed in an educational environment which is noncompetitive. Similarly, a *formal* structure may develop values markedly different from those developed in an *informal* instructional structure. Certain procedures may be more authoritarian in structure than others, each cultivating different standards.

The point here is that each educational alternative produces a type of social system, including a system of social control, which, in turn, influences the valuing behavior of those within its boundaries. A child placed in a rigid, authoritarian social structure is not likely to learn democratic values. Rather, those environments which themselves are democratic are most likely to develop democratic values.

While educational options are desirable because they do offer more choice, they must also be judged by their impact upon the value development of the next generation of citizens. If we want adults who are self-directing, compassionate toward their fellow man, socially concerned, respectful of differing cultures and styles, and dedicated to the other "humane" values we are likely to associate with democracy, our educational options will have to create processes in which these values are in actual operation in the schools.

All of us who exercise choice among educational alternatives will do well to keep the question of values directly before us.

EVALUATING PUBLIC SCHOOLS OF CHOICE

Evaluation, therefore, becomes an integral, important part of Public Schools of Choice. When there are diverse roads to common ends, we must all know how well those who take each road are progressing toward those ends. Two kinds of evaluation are likely to take place. The first type of evaluation will be done by the participants themselves on a continuing basis. As information is uncovered, it is immediately fed back into the process, so that the information can be used to improve the situation. For example, in one of the alternatives, say, an open classroom, parents begin to feel concern that the basic skills are not being sufficiently emphasized. This information is at once brought back to the teacher to be used to improve the overall "open classroom" approach. The second type of evaluation is an administrative assessment of the overall impact of the alternative in relation to the common set of educational objectives. These data become public so that all can see what is happening to the total program.

Naturally, there are difficulties—methodologically—with most evaluations. Controlled experiments are difficult in the actual public schools because of their dynamic nature. There simply are no reliable and valid instruments for assessing certain kinds of objectives, for example, for measuring how a learner feels about himself.

However, alternative educational environments should stimulate new modes of assessment; e.g., having anthropologists "live" in different educational environments, as they would in different cultures. An anthropologist could, as a participant, observe and give an assessment based on his own discipline. A child psychologist could do the same, and so on.

Since we are dealing with different educational alternatives, each with its own distinct cultural environment, new assessment patterns need to be mounted lest particular alternatives be given preference by the type of evaluation utilized. Since the standard educational option has had the most experience, it is natural that evaluation procedures have been developed to measure its effectiveness. Standardized tests do, after all, reflect the established pattern of public education.

It is likely that in the future more *longitudinal* evaluations will take place, not unlike the "Eight Year Study" of the 1930's. At that time, an eight-year evaluation design was developed, aimed at measuring the differences between "progressive" and "conventional" school graduates. This study followed two groups of graduates to determine how they performed in college. Chamberlain and others report on the results:

The experiment might have been judged in many different ways; after all, the ultimate proof of an education is in the lives people lead when they have left the classroom. But the commission was determined to test the results in terms of how well graduates of the thirty schools performed in college. Under . . . Ralph W. Tyler, of the University of Chicago, a team of measurement experts set out to compare these graduates with other college students with similar background and ability. The team's technique was to set up 1,475 pairs of college students, each consisting of a graduate of one of the thirty schools and a graduate of some other secondary school matched as closely as possible with respect to sex, age, race, scholastic aptitude, scores, home and community background, and vocational and avocational interests.

. . . The evaluation team found that graduates of the thirty schools (1) earned a slightly higher total grade average; (2) received slightly more academic honors in each of the four years; (3) seemed to possess a higher degree of intellectual curiosity and drive; (4) seemed to be more precise, systematic, and objective in their thinking; (5) seemed to have developed clearer ideas concerning . . . education; (6) more often demonstrated a high degree of resourcefulness in meeting new situations; (7) had about the same problems of adjustment as the comparison group but approached their solution with greater effectiveness; (8) participated more and more frequently in organized student groups; (9) earned a higher percentage of non-academic honors; (10) had a somewhat better orientation toward choice of vocation; and (11) demonstrated a more active concern with national and world affairs.*

Much of the evaluation associated with Public Schools of Choice must be based on consumer satisfaction. Since the essence of this plan is individual choice, it is to the individual that evaluation is ultimately directed. Parents who express satisfaction with the progress that their child is making have made important evaluative judgments.

Summarizing the results of a four-year study which analyzed data of previous research dealing with the effects of schooling, Mary Jo Bane and Christopher S. Jencks report:

. . . the primary basis for evaluating a school should be whether the students and teachers find it a satisfying place to be . . .†

* D. Chamberlain, et al. "Did They Succeed in College?" in L. A. Cremen, *The Transformation of the School.* New York: Knopf, 1961, pp. 255–6.

† Mary Jo Bane and Christopher S. Jencks, "The Schools and Equal Opportunity," in *Saturday Review of Education*, Sept. 16, 1972, p. 41.

One of the major reasons for having alternatives within the framework of public schools is to protect the family from consumer fraud. Because public schools are accountable to the immediate community and the state for standards, it is likely that educational alternatives there will be developed with more quality control than might be the case in private schools. While some may argue that private schools offer more freedom, it is also true that this freedom can be abused to compromise quality. All the way from safety regulations to certification of professional personnel, public schools have mandated requirements. While the public schools may take longer to develop alternatives, they are also more likely to be of the caliber that protects the consumer. Once public schools concentrate their resources on alternatives, the problem of quality can be tackled squarely. For example, professional personnel who need to be retrained can be required to undertake retraining; school budgets already contain line-items on staff development and in-service training. These may be used to prepare personnel to mount the educational alternatives being offered.

At this time the public schools, having more resources than private schools, are better able to offer quality educational alternatives that mediate against consumer fraud. It is possible also that we may eventually include alternative private schools in an expanded public school framework.

However, any broad evaluation program must maintain regular visits from "outside" experts who can give testimony to parents, teachers, and students of the quality of each alternate.

The American tradition of free public school is being seriously challenged because it cannot, as presently structured, deal effectively with both diversity and the demand for compulsory education. It is attempting to force each member of our very diverse student population to adjust to the *one* process offered or be branded as a failure. Teachers also are imprisoned by uniformity. Their own distinctive styles of teaching need to be liberated. Different styles of teaching make up different forms of education. Such styles can become educational options by which learning can be motivated by choice. It is time that we redefined, reconceptualized, *public* education to include alternatives which heretofore have not been available by choice, e.g., open schools, multicultural schools, Montessori schools, college preparatory schools, and the like.

We are not suggesting the replacement of the traditional public school. The present educational system claims to possess the ingredients necessary for quality education, and points to the millions of individuals who have been successfully educated in public schools. The standard school is certainly *one* alternative of quality education. However, it is no longer a suitable alternative for growing numbers of teachers, parents and students. We need to expand the options for all these people—not by exclusions, but by inclusions. If increased numbers of students, parents, and other citizens want alternatives to the standard school and standard program, their options need not take the form of private school, parochial school or require moving to another region of the country. (Even if one undertook to move to a different community or region, he would have to pinpoint his move to a particular school in a particular neighborhood.)

The present strategy of reform is across-the-board: the same for everybody. Little or no consideration is given to individual differences among teachers, parents and students. The fallacy of this reasoning should be obvious. While one option may make sense for one party—for teachers or for parents or for students—it may not meet the needs or answer the concerns of the other groups. Usually one group, the most powerful, imposes its ideas on the others, and thus sows the seeds of conflict. For example, during the 30's and 40's many professional educators embraced "progressive education" as the preferable process and tried to implement "progressive education" programs, only to have the other parties of interest—parents, citizens, and in many cases, the students themselves—reject it. In other instances, innovations were introduced by the administration without the consent of any of the parties of interest. For any new approach to work, the educational proposal has to bring together the major parties of interest as a foundation for reform. This means that the learner (or his peer group), the professional and the parents all have to be at the decision-gate together.

The public school system of choice that we propose is a supply-and-demand model, but it differs very significantly from other supply-and-demand or consumer models that have been proposed. Some models have proposed that the parent be given tuition vouchers equivalent to the total per-pupil cost to enable him to shop around for the kind of education he wants, so that he may move into a private school if that type of education makes sense to him. Such shopping around is fine, but it is done at considerable inconvenience to the consumer, whereas, under Public Schools of Choice, the public schools themselves would become responsive to the concerns of the consumer, and would translate those concerns into programs at the local public school level. The Choice system attempts to update the public schools that have traditionally served the needs of an open society. It is because we are entering a new period, a new age, that our educational system must be updated. The Public Schools of Choice approach retains the overall conception of public education, legitimizes under this umbrella educational options that have heretofore been available only outside the public school system, and makes these options available through free choice by the consumer. Since the alternatives are based on different styles of teaching, the teacher, under Public Schools of Choice, is freed from the restrictions imposed by a uniform system. He or she too selects the alternative that is most compatible with his or her style of teaching.

IV / BERKELEY'S ALTERNATE
SCHOOLS PLAN

The Berkeley School System in California was the first to launch a full-scale version of Public Schools of Choice.* The Berkeley community was the perfect place for such an experiment, since its ethnic composition is markedly diverse—48.4 percent white, 43.7 percent black, 7.9 percent other minorities—and its cultural

* Much of the material for this chapter is based on personal visits to the Berkeley School System, on private conversations with key personnel, and on individual letters. I have also made use of the following publications: *Berkeley School Report #15*, June 1971; *Experimental Schools Program Report* of the U.S. Department of Health, Education and Welfare/Office of Education, U.S. Printing Office, 1972; *Description of Berkeley's Alternative Schools*, released by the Experimental Schools Support Office; *Experimental Schools in Berkeley*, Berkeley Unified School District, September, 1971; *Alternative Education*, a publication of the Experimental Schools Program in Berkeley, published in October, 1972.

I am extremely grateful to the Berkeley Unified School District for allowing me to reprint sections of these two documents: *Options Through Participation* (August 3, 1970) and *Alternate Schools of Education Experimental Schools Program* (April 6, 1971).

climate is extraordinarily sophisticated. The presence of the University of California campus adds considerably to the progressive atmosphere.

In the summer of 1968, two projects were in operation in the Berkeley Unified School System which were destined to affect not only the Berkeley school district, but the nation's schools as well. One, called "Summer Project," was a program aimed at high school youngsters; two drama teachers from the high school spearheaded this effort, which attempted to maximize student self-expression. The second was a project headed by Herbert Kohl, author of *36 Children*.* With the help of a Carnegie Corporation grant, Kohl was looking for a new home for his largely off-beat teacher training program, which he was calling "Other Ways." Kohl and his colleagues had developed an "open," student-centered secondary school. His tightly knit staff had agreed to work for no more than $100 a week each.

Both projects turned into "experimental secondary schools." "Summer Project" became Community High School, a school for over 225 students. The "Other Ways" project became a Grade 7 to Grade 12 school for close to a hundred racially diverse students.

The distinctive educational programs which evolved from each of these experiments signaled further possibilities to the pluralistic Berkeley Community, ripe as it was for educational options.

During the 1968–69 school year there was a change in the Berkeley School superintendency. Neil V. Sullivan, under whom the Berkeley Unified School System had been desegregated, left. His replacement was Dick Foster. It was Foster who provided the administrative leadership for the development of an alternative school system for Berkeley.

Alternative education in the Berkeley district began in February of 1969 when Jay Manley, drama teacher at Berkeley

* Herbert Kohl, *36 Children*, New York, New American Library, 1967.

High, headed up a sub-school located at first in a second-floor cluster of rooms in the Community Theatre on campus. It was a spin-off mini-school named Community High and had been a year in the planning. It began when Manley and other teachers got together on the need for an option to the regular offering at Berkeley High. Considerable negotiations with the administration took place before the experiment finally got under way. In the fall of 1969, Community High was relocated into the corridors of the Community Theatre. By this time, Other Ways had come into being. Other Ways was an off-site effort at "turning on" youths who couldn't and/or wouldn't cope with the regular system.*

With Kohl now proposing that his Other Ways become an alternative *within* the structure of the Berkeley Public Schools —that is, that it be supported by public, not private, money— Foster became immediately involved with alternative education. He named Kohl principal of the Other Ways School.

Once Kohl's Other Ways was legitimized as a public school, the road was open for other options. Both Kohl and Foster sought outside "seed" money to develop other educational alternatives. Because Berkeley was the first major public school system to propose a full-scale alternatives program, it became the focus for outside private and public support; it was a prototype district from which others might learn. The Ford Foundation awarded the district a $250,000 grant in 1970. This grant enabled Berkeley to stabilize its initial alternatives, while also preparing an expanded program of options. In April 1971, Berkeley qualified for a grant from the newly established Experimental Schools Program of the United States Office of Education and was awarded a thirty-month grant of $3,637,563.† With this additional funding, the Berkeley Unified School District ex-

---

* *Alternative Education*, a publication of the Experimental Schools Program in Berkeley, October, 1972.
† *Experimental Schools Program Report*, cited above, 1971.

panded its educational alternatives program to over twenty distinct options for parents, students and staff.*

The two original alternatives—Community High School and Other Ways (both renamed)—are now in full operation. Community High School, now renamed Genesis (Berkeley's first alternative), with over one hundred sixty students in racially balanced numbers, was organized during the first year into four "tribes" in which close, individualized contacts were maintained between teachers and students. Each semester the students negotiate their own programs. Among the hundred and fifty courses which have been offered are Photography, Black Economics, and Survival Crafts. Like many of the other options, Genesis provides students and community residents with a greater voice in educational decision-making than they have ever before had. For instance, an Inter-Tribal Council consisting of student, parent and staff representatives governs the school.

During its third year, the entire alternative called Genesis was reshaped because "the early Community High appeared to have gone too far into a 'do your own thing' stance . . . with the stigma of being a 'free, hippie-type' hangout for youths who don't want to work." †

The staff rethought the entire program including its governance structure, staff and administration:

Genesis is governed by a community of students, parents and staff. Curriculum is tighter and there's more in it to do with mastery of reading and math. There's strong attention to differences springing from the different racial and ethnic experiences.

Community High has long lived with the stigma of being mostly for whites. The upheaval last year was over that issue as staff and students really tried to figure out why mostly white students opted for that alternative.

* These are now listed in the *Experimental Schools Program Report*, cited above, U.S. Office of Education publication, p. 16.

† From *Alternative Education*, a publication of the Experimental Schools Program in Berkeley, October 1972, p. 19.

It must be, they decided, because the offering in it speaks mainly to whites.

The offering began to change last year as a cross-cultural course giving an awareness of what it's like to be of a minority race became required for all students and as staff encountered the issue of institutional racism.

Other Ways, now renamed Marcus Garvey Institute, is located in a large old building that the students and staff themselves brought up to school code. The school is informally structured and offers a wide range of subjects, focusing on psychological, urban, financial, social and political survival themes. Much of the curriculum is reality-based, emphasizing learning by doing. For instance, several students are engaged in building a schooner. In the process, they are learning navigational principles which rely heavily on an understanding of math and science concepts. Full scale apprenticeships are maintained also in such places as law offices, pottery studios and book stores.

During its first year of operation, in 1969, families that considered the Other Ways option were interviewed, along with the prospective student, by the staff. I happened to be with Herb Kohl one evening (before the name change) when he interviewed two families whose sons were interested in Other Ways. Kohl made sure that the student and his family understood the program. He was interested in the student's own motivation, in whether he was really attracted to the Other Ways educational approach. Kohl asked many questions, projecting the sense that he and his colleagues were not simply taking everyone who asked to come, but were favoring those whose motivation and style connected with the Other Ways educational environment.

The family appeared interested in the program. They were eager to find an alternative that could make contact with their adolescent son, who obviously was not responding fully to the standard junior high program. They seemed pleased, even grateful, that options—middle-class options—did exist for them to consider.

During the summer of 1971 and continuing into the next year, a restructuring of the program took place. A new director was named. In February of 1972, the alternative was renamed in honor of Marcus Garvey and his philosophy of self-determination. A new staff was engaged for the school. Most of the school's students are now nonwhite. The project is zeroing in on the problem of how minorities can deal with the effects of institutional racism, and also on the structured delivery of basic reading and mathematics skills. There is a two-part instructional approach—heavy stress on the basics, and stress as well on ethnic culture. The staff at Garvey see this alternative as a survival center.

One of the "Tribes" in the Community High School split off in 1971 to become *Alliance Black House*—an option that emphasizes "black identity." This move was led by one of the black teachers, the late Buddy Jackson, who felt that the program as it then existed was not designed to meet the needs of black youth. Housed in a YMCA, this alternative attracted over sixty tenth and eleventh graders. There are no failures at Alliance Black House. If a student does not earn a passing grade, he is simply given no credit. The black experience is the distinctive feature of the curriculum. Blacks who have experienced racism and its consequences—isolation, powerlessness, low achievement—become concerned with the problem of self-esteem and with helping their black brothers through "classrooms" out in the community, in courtrooms, prisons, churches, and so on. Note the description of Alliance Black House:

Students, about sixty during the 1971 school year, turned the cavernous and unlovely facility on Fourth Street into an arts center with their huge murals that strikingly chronicle the black experience. As the walls filled up with the artistic outpouring of students growing in understanding of themselves, Black House grew into a unified learning place with a clear set of goals.

When Black House opened for the 1972-73 school year, the history of becoming a particular place for a particular group of students was reflected in a tightly structured curriculum with a heavy priority on mastery of basic skills.

For two hours each morning these courses are taught: reading and writing, Black studies, general math, Black man and the law, Black literature, chemistry, and political science. The afternoon curriculum includes arts and crafts, geometry, algebra, chemistry, Spanish, Afro-Asian dance, Swahili, boxing, biology and nutritional sciences. Most subjects are offered on a six-week rather than semester basis.

In reading, writing and math, teachers work in teams. Each student is diagnosed as to exactly where he is in terms of academic strengths and weaknesses.[*]

A black staff steeped in black consciousness interacts with the students. While much of the curriculum is basic and offers all the required high school courses, the school is also concerned with the *identity-building* process which is maximized by the staff.

In the fall of 1972, an alliance was created among Black House and two other alternatives (Casa de la Raza and Odyssey). This alliance makes it possible for these options to share resources.[†]

In the spring of 1971, a class in Contemporary Problems in Education at Willard Junior High grew into an option called Odyssey. Located in a Lutheran Church, it now enrolls about ninety junior high youngsters of grades seven through nine. These youngsters have spent a year working out a multiracial program. Several projects have been mounted, including the construction of a geodesic dome and the staging of a Malcolm X festival. Black Studies, Nature Study, Creative Writing, and Community Service are part of the program. Volunteers assist in the learning process, with talent available from the community, including the University of California.

Like the other options described here, Odyssey offers per-

[*] *Ibid.*, p. 8.
[†] *Ibid.*, p. 8.

sonalized learning, with considerable emphasis on workshoplike projects.

The main campus of Berkeley High School, once the only alternative available to the community, has, as we have seen, been subdivided. These units are being continued through 1972–73.

In the fall of 1971 *East Campus*, involving 175 students in grades 9 to 12, was organized. After an unsuccessful start on the main high school campus and a period in Sunclous along Grove Street, the school is now located on part of the school district's Savo Island property. The curriculum focuses on basic skills, with great emphasis placed on attending daily. A work apprenticeship program is in operation, as is an evening program for students who have financial or family responsibilities and cannot attend during the day.

Many services are provided *East Campus* students by the school's staff of twelve teachers, four college students and four volunteers. Parents are interviewed when the child enrolls, and regular parent meetings are held during the year. Teacher-advisers also hold regular meetings with students, engage in biweekly schoolwide meetings and make home visits. The school provides intensive counseling, as well as an eleven-month year, with residential facilities for those who might profit from such arrangements. A World of Work arrangement provides part-time employment for students, and a Media Center helps students learn independently. Increasingly, students are making the decisions relating to their education. The commitment to the learner is emphasized:

Perhaps the most special thing about *East Campus* is the open-ended commitment to any youth who needs the school. When a youth leaves, he is told to return if he needs to. Students have been taken in long after enrollment was at the preferred peak of 150. If the staff can't find another school where the student would have a chance of making it, they take him, despite the devotion to smallness as being one of the ways to maintain a personal and caring school.

If a student is dropped from *East Campus* because he won't show up or won't perform in any way, the door is still open. One student recently returned after a two-week absence, asked and was granted readmission, and proceeded to take care of the business of getting the education he needed so there would be a future for him.*

Model A School, which started in February 1970, is a structured skills-oriented subschool of 400 students in grades 10–12, housed on the Berkeley High School Campus in a string of adjoining classrooms on the second floor. In addition to mastery of basic skills—including the use of math labs—the tenth grade curriculum emphasizes *The Study of Man,* a course in which knowledge of the different cultures of the world and their approaches to common goals is the central subject. The eleventh grade emphasizes *American Culture* and the contributions of diverse elements of the population to the formation of American society. This description of *Model A* gives us a taste of its flavor.

The offering includes Hindu myths and legends, geography of China, Taoism, Greek lyric poetry, African family structure, Renaissance man as the source of order and disorder, Shakespeare, Chinese jade carving, Bunraku puppet theatre, rise of the middle class.

Tutorial centers were set up which have become a strength and a model of the program. In double periods daily, students in need of upgrading in reading achievement are in the centers. They move then to the math labs.

The centers have become impressive learning stations. Model A, through evolution, has become two places—one where a refined and richly honed academic offering is served up in heavy doses and teachers work together and combine students regularly each week so that the offering in fact becomes unfrozen and flows—English into history, science into math—and the whole thing into a profile of the life man has lived since the beginning of his time.

While this is going on, the 40 percent of the Model A student body who need it are getting drill and tutorial one-to-one help in a living-roomlike setting that is supportive and comfortable. Aides are stationed in the centers. The climate is almost familylike. In this milieu

* *Ibid.,* p. 16.

of people taking care of their futures by getting the basic academic tools, students in the past year have shot up two, three and four grade levels.*

The student body of *Model A* is heterogeneous as to race and ability.

The *Agora* is another sub-unit of Berkeley High School, occupying a wing of the school. In a school for one hundred racially diverse students and teachers, the students are equally divided among black, Chicano, white and Asian races. *Agora* is intended to reach those who are failing, bored or disenchanted with the school system. Students choose their own classes and teachers. They also participate in the planning and development of the school, including the setting of rules and policies.

Instructional emphasis here is on mastery of basic skills, especially communication skills. The manageable size of the *Agora* enables it to develop in its students a sense of community which enhances the security of the participants.

As with most of the other options, the *Agora* maintains strong community ties, with direct school-parent contact achieved through home visitation and parent participation in school affairs, including policy formation. Also:

Classes at Agora include Harlem Renaissance and what it's like, geometry, language—tool or weapon, Chicano studies, algebra, communication skills, basic design, Black seminar, soccer, modern and Afro dance, math games, art work shop, Black drama, American folk lore, creative writing, women's studies, chess, Mexican folk dance, music performance, Spanish, international cooking, human awareness and tennis.

Agora has become the place students were asking for in the summer of 1970 when all those meetings were held from the Community High waiting list—an educational alternative where students have the say.†

* *Ibid.*, p. 31.
† *Ibid.*, p. 6.

School of the Arts is another unit (220 students) located in the Community Theatre of the High School. Catering to students who have artistic inclinations or who are seeking a broad, cultural approach, the integrated curriculum combines art, dance, drama, music, TV, radio, film-making and communication skills, with an English-History-Humanities core. Only about half the students are now in the Performing Arts Department, the division that created the school.

Certain required courses—math, science and physical education—are taken at the main high school. A typical day is described:

An example of a day in the life of a School of the Arts student is: He starts his day in SA with the Children's Theatre Workshop. He goes then to the regular high school for math, back to School of the Arts for orchestra or concert chorale, back to the main school for biology and on again to SA for Israeli folk dance. He stays at School of the Arts for his last period of the day, art of American politics and law.

Offerings in School of the Arts include comedy in art and drama, creative writing, reading skills, electronic piano lab, English composition, music history, the American mind, cultural experience, environment, mythology, jazz, chamber singing, rock-soul instrumental, symphonic ensemble, marching and stage band, acting, stagecraft, costume production, photography, radio journalism and fencing.

All students of School of the Arts come together once a week to share what they have learned with each other and to get to know each other through their common interest in the arts.*

Berkeley College Preparatory is a school for 50 sophomores and juniors. Teachers and paraprofessionals reflect the ethnic and racial composition of the student body. The college preparatory curriculum is Afro-oriented. Traditional social studies, English, foreign languages and other required courses are emphasized. Courses in the special areas—science, math, physical education—are given at the regular high school building.

* *Ibid.*, p. 33.

To be in Berkeley College Prep, a student must take 15 units in the program. The 17-class curriculum comprises the traditional college prep courses (math, English and social studies) taught from an African-American perspective.

A major stress is on preparing students for the taking of tests. All juniors take the PSAT/National Merit twice during the school year, and seniors the SAT. Teachers serve also as counselors, advising students on needed courses and helping them find out about outside programs that further meet their needs. Approximately 40 students will get additional tutoring help this year in the after-school neighborhood learning centers.*

A 16-member student advisory board has been formed as an initial policy group that will work with staff and parents.

The *On Target School* (OTS) is still another subdivision (grades 10–12) of Berkeley High School. It opened in the fall of 1971. Its 140 culturally diverse students are involved in a program that has a clear career orientation. Industry-education councils are formed to maximize student success in the workworld. With the assistance of the business and industrial community, the *On Target* School provides students with real on-the-job experiences.

At *On Target* the academic disciplines are integrated around the student's career interests, through a block scheduling of formal courses. First-hand experiences in business, industry and educational institutions have a heavy science and technology emphasis. Students have an opportunity to develop their talents and relate them to suitable career options. The school tries to equip each learner with the skills necessary for success in his career choice. The program aspects of OTS are described as follows:

Most *On Target* students take three courses in the alternative and they are all involved in the frequent field trips to such occupation

* *Ibid.*, p. 13.

centers as airports, hospitals, banks, plants and industries to see how the jobs are actually performed.

OTS classes include biology, physiology, physics, chemistry, algebra, trigonometry, geometry, computer programming, shorthand, model office, bookkeeping, typing and pre-nursing.

The OTS experience is a combination of these classes, the field trips, practice in test-taking, vocational counseling, learning experiences in both the Computer and Career Centers and assemblies in which guest speakers describe requirements for work in industries, business and vocations.

On Target is not a self-contained alternative. The remainder of the students' class work is taken in the regular Berkeley High School program.*

Berkeley has two junior high schools, King and Willard. Both were without alternatives until the fall of 1972 when options developed in both schools.

At King Junior High School, the option developed was called *KARE* (King's Alternative for Relevant Education). This is a school within a school, composed of 140 students. The smallness of the unit allows the staff to deal with children in a more personal way.

The program at KARE is described as follows:

Subjects in KARE include English, which takes in creative writing, grammar, composition, speech and discussion, journalism, etc.; the social studies unit called "People and Technology" and supplemented with units in contemporary problems, history, geography and city government; math, taught at three levels—skills, theory and accelerated math; science, which includes general science, astronomy, earth science, ecology and biology; a comprehensive reading program provided with the High Intensity Learning System; physical education, which takes in tumbling, football, soccer, Afro-Asian dance, tennis, yoga, karate and wrestling.

Typing is taught as a personal-use course and also reinforces the language arts skills. A Career Resource Center will enable students to assess their own interests and aptitudes for future work.

* *Ibid.*, p. 32.

A prime ingredient of the course offering at KARE is ethnic studies. It is taught in three sections and from three perspectives—Afro-American, Asian and majority-minority relations. Each section is a semester long and students not in the course one semester are strongly encouraged to take it the next because it relates to a main purpose of KARE—increased understanding, people to people.*

The *Willard Alternative* for 150 students is aimed at trying to give students a greater responsibility over their lives.

When students first get to school in the morning, they have fifteen minutes of talk in their first class, a type of "debugging" session aimed at freeing up the student for a day of learning.

For the remainder of a typical day:

. . . it's a whole morning of math-science and English-history. This puts the school day at 12:30, when it's time for an elective. Choices within the alternative are creative games, social living (required of 8th graders) or a tutorial study session. The students can opt instead into an elective in the regular Willard program.

After lunch, the offering is a choice of creative writing, drama, arts-crafts, typing or gospel choir. The last period of the day is a choice of cycling, karate, football, basketball, swimming, soccer, track, volley ball or ping pong.†

West Campus Basic Skills is a grade 9 option. A massive attack on the basic skills for any student who is behind is the intent of this school. In February 1973, this alternative opened with 75 students who will also have a daily program of field experiences.

The students will also be connected with the United States Office of Education program Right to Read, an after-school program at West Campus.

A careful assessment program will accompany each student in an attempt to develop academic growth on a continuous basis.‡

* *Ibid.*, pp. 25–26.
† *Ibid.*, p. 39.
‡ *Ibid.*, p. 34.

West Campus Career Exploration is a ninth grade option for 100 students. As the name suggests, the theme of this option is careers. Susan Lum, who directs the program, gives her view of this alternative school:

Major goal is to provide in-depth exploration and expanding opportunities for all students to develop attitudes, interests and skills which will help them to choose wisely and realistically both in their own educational careers and in the constantly changing career market and, of course, to see the relationship between the two.

Hospitals, city government, recreational agencies, business, industry, and the performing arts will be among the areas from which the students may choose. The students will select one major career and then devote at least an hour a day in exploration and training throughout that area. Students in Career Exploration will receive academic credit. With the help of teachers and college students, the students will design a study program at *West Campus* which complements their field work. The college students will also serve as liaison between students, employers and school staff.

Since this alternative requires the ability to adjust to a varied schedule and since there is no basic skill component devised for the starting year, we are seeking students who like to work on their own, who won't be jeopardized or penalized by absence from regular basic skills classes, and who have or can develop a sense of responsibility.

The major purpose of this program is to enable our students to set realistic and knowledgeable goals for themselves and then to embark upon a program of preparation to attain such goals.*

The *West Campus Work Study* is a ninth grade school for 50 students. This option provides students with an opportunity to move to the main campus at midsemester after concentrated study and attention at the *West Campus*. The small size of the groupings here allows for intensive individualized assistance from a small self-selected staff.

Students at *West Campus* are likely to learn such basic skills as getting to school on time and following through on assign-

* *Ibid.,* p. 35.

ments. The academic skills are given priority. Work experiences have become an integral part of the curriculum, with work-study opportunities occupying most of the afternoon hours.

West Campus is a kind of "halfway house" in which students who find it difficult to adjust to the main campus are provided with a transitional environment in which to retool.

West Campus HUI, formerly *Multicultural High Potential*, is the name given to a ninth grade unit of 100 culturally diverse students: white, black, and Oriental. *HUI* is a Chinese term meaning "come together" or "work together." In addition to the multicultural emphasis, this alternative school encourages personal self-direction.

Opportunities for tutoring are provided. Each student and teacher keeps a diary, and there are frequent sessions for joint assessments of personal growth, as well as of program direction. HUI is described by the Berkeley United School District:

> Most students take three or more classes in HUI and the balance in the common school. HUI's major subjects include English, Social Science, math, science, foreign language and P. E.
> In addition to a heavy academic emphasis, HUI stresses: (1) sharing of ideas, techniques, materials, (2) development of interdisciplinary programs, (3) opportunities for interchange among the students and the faculty, (4) learning experiences to reach the fullest capacity of HUI students, personally and intellectually.
> Since West Campus is a one-year campus, normally the entire student body moves each year. To promote continuity, HUI is broadening its scope, and 25 sophomores now continue at West Campus, making it a two-year alternative.*

A kindergarten-through-grade-12 school for eighty-five students—this one emphasizing Chicano culture—is *Alliance Casa de la Raza*, located at King Junior High and in adjacent bungalows:

* *Ibid.*, p. 36.

In the last days of the 1972 summer vacation, the bungalows on King Junior High School campus that comprise Casa de la Raza were filled with parents and community persons at work to make that school ready for the students who would soon descend into the set of adjacent wooden rooms on the school's backyard. Many of the parents working to paint the walls, lay carpet, clean the windows, had more than one child in school.

This is a central feature of Casa—a family place. With the ambitious grade structure spanning everything from kindergarten through high school, families can have all their children in one school—and one based on their life experience as Chicanos. Interlaced in the link of family ties are the strains of ethnic and cultural roots and experiences.*

A bilingual, nongraded school, this alternative has a strong Spanish heritage component. Cultural studies, including religion, folklore, crafts, magic and fine arts, are offered. A 36-member board (staff, students and parents) makes most of the decisions for the school.

Science and mathematics are taught by bilingual teaching methods. The curriculum includes service activities related to community health and legal problems.

The school is organized around a "family" concept, with about 50 families now involved in the operation.

With a waiting list of over 300 parents wanting to get their children into *Early Learning Center* (ELC), the need for this alternative is clear. In 1972, this option started with 75 students. During the second year another 75 students were admitted. In the planning which preceded the implementation of this alternative (July 1971 to June 1972), the community was surveyed to identify individuals with special talents who could relate to children of elementary school age, and a resource pool was developed. The flexible nature of this option is described:

* *Ibid.*, p. 9.

The main effort at ELC is to build a flexible and open community school. If pupils spend three days on a camp trip, they could spend the next three days at home. There are no bells in the school. The hope is that learning activities will flow into each other, that the youngsters can stay at a pursuit until they want to leave it, that people in the community will come to the school and share their skills and talent with the children.

Staff wants to break down the separateness between school and the world around it and school and home.*

A group of parents of children of elementary school age, together with several teachers, formed the *Parents and Teachers for Alternative Education* (PTAE) now called *Kilimanjaro*. This group of about fifty parents, students and teachers from two elementary schools sought and achieved a learning environment that was more spontaneous than the standard educational offering. Located apart from the elementary school, Kilimanjaro has developed a nongraded elementary format, and is open to community resources. The student body is multiracial and multiethnic in composition.

Wide use is made of parent involvement in the school. Parents learn along with their children. The curriculum emerges from the interaction of the basic parties of interest (children, parents, teachers, community). The participants make full use as well of community resources, such as the university, museums, parks, craftsmen, artists and older students. Children in Kilimanjaro cook, weave, make pottery, garden and learn the basic skills in an environment which is open and informal.

The place finally found for the Kilimanjaro home is somehow very right, and symbolic. In the midst of the near-palatial hill section skirting the north side of the U. C. campus—an area that bespeaks societal luxury and the richness that material acquisition can bring—in this midst sits the Kilimanjaro cluster of sweetly defiant folk who insert their motley, free spirit presence into the affluent scene.

The red brick former church has been shaped to the likes of kids.

* *Ibid.*, p. 14.

The environs are bedecked with the creative output of a flock of children who have been let loose to do what they want. As it turns out, the kids have been very purposeful—highly creative, fast to grow in skills to do the things that please them. They write booklets on a frequent and consistent basis; they build and paint and draw and fashion from clay and glass and metal. They sing and recite and write plays.

When given a free rein, they work very hard.*

The kindergarten-to-grade-3 *John Muir Child Development Center* for nearly 400 students grew out of a strong parent-teacher interest in child development. This twelve-month school offers parents further options, which they themselves help generate, within the Center itself. Parents are closely involved in the child's school experiences. Each classroom has a number of learning centers in science, math and language arts. The social studies curriculum has a strong ethnic studies emphasis. This is an "open" school:

The point of the Child Development Center is to provide the material and equipment for learning and let the child loose to work at the activity stations where his interests lie. The "open" classroom, then, is a place where the learner chooses a subject and learns through doing.

Characteristic of the John Muir alternative is an air of heightened bustle—kids hammering, kilns whirling, rehearsals, music—the sounds, sights and smells of children who seem to have meshed work and play into one and the same phenomena.†

The child development thrust here provides a curriculum developed around the interests, curiosity and spontaneity of the learner. A strong music, dance and motor development program is maintained.

"The environment" is the central theme of *the Malcolm X Environmental Studies Program* formerly the *Lincoln Environ-*

* *Ibid.,* pp. 27–28.
† *Ibid.,* pp. 23–24.

mental Studies Project. A new school for 90 students from grades four to six, this option undertakes an exploration of the physical and home environment of each student. In the process, the students learn basic skills and develop computational know-how, as well as relating to the other academic areas.

Paraprofessionals from the community are utilized to diversify the program. In the mornings, the class concentrates on skills; the afternoons are devoted to activity projects. Two afternoons are spent on such social issues as community organization, civil disobedience and drug abuse. Twice a week students opt to study drama, philosophy, music, sewing, cooking, etc. A description of this alternative states:

It's a creative place—the basement wing of Malcolm X where the series of classrooms that house Environmental Studies are located. The classrooms don't really contain the students—the environs of the Bay Area do. Last year it was Carmel Valley and Sacramento County and Yosemite.

The idea is to take the kids where their interests are and to turn the results of their interests into the curriculum, with careful attention to intensive upgrading of reading and math skills.*

The *Franklin Multicultural School,* begun in fall 1971, is a school for 300 fourth to sixth grade students (out of a total Franklin student population of 970). In order to combat institutionalized racism (a theme for all Berkeley's alternatives), this unit systematically arranges to have students of different cultural backgrounds interact with one another to become aware of and respond to their own distinctive cultural heritage. This alternative grew out of a community concern for the special needs of Asians in this district.

Students are organized into an Asian cluster and Multicultural model. The Asian cluster serves 120 students; the Multicultural model has over 200 students.

* *Ibid.,* p. 29.

This is also a bilingual alternative. Asian classes are in operation, emphasizing Asian language and culture. Multicultural classes, with children from all the cultural groups, concentrate on increasing the learner's understanding and appreciation of different cultures.

Over 60 tutors from the University of California are assigned to this alternative.

Both components share features in common. These include: small groups for reading instruction; personalized approach to the children and their learning needs; use of UC reading tutors; individualized counseling by teachers; openness to parents; heavy use of multicultural materials and origination by the teachers themselves of curriculum; frequent cultural field trips; use of team teaching and of classroom instructional aides; stress on life-related activities such as producing magazines and newspapers, building projects, conducting classroom banks, stores, libraries, courts, radio programs, movies, dramatic performances, farms, landscaping and cooking.

The Asian cluster has all races. Asian teachers and aides relate the perspective of their racial life experiences to the basic class subjects.

In both components there is an attempt to tailor-make the offering to the human wealth the children bring to school with them.*

Over 650 children, kindergarten through grade three, attend *Jefferson Tri-Part Model,* a school-within-a-school. Parents at Jefferson have access to three distinctive forms of education, or, more accurately, they have a choice of three options:

1) The Multicultural model in which cultural diversity is cultivated
2) The Individualized, Personalized, Learning model (IPL) with a self-instructional mode
3) The Traditional model with a teacher-directed pattern

Student enrollments for these three models are: Multicultural, 240; Individualized Personalized Learning, 210; Traditional, 115.

* *Ibid.,* p. 17.

A staff senate has been created, chaired by a staff member. The three sub-units are described as follows:

The three models offer roughly what their titles connote. Traditional is where the teacher is the prime giver of knowledge and the lecturer-receiver relationship is a basis of the instruction. It doesn't mean, however, that there is not individualization when needed or multiculturalism when the subject matter relates to it. It's a process of imparting knowledge and it's one with which many parents and teachers are comfortable and some children need.

The individualized group strives to find out where each child is and tailor-make the learning program to that point—not to view him as a class group but as a unique and different individual. The multicultural cluster runs the study-of-man theme through the curriculum, stressing the specialness and contributions of the various cultures. There's a lot of creative outpouring from the students and many cultural excursions as well as a Heritage House which is like a live cultural museum. The multicultural model also includes a choice of Chinese and Spanish bilingual classes. These grew out of needs expressed by parents.*

ORGANIZATION AND IMPLEMENTATION
OF ALTERNATIVE SCHOOLS

Over twenty alternatives, involving over five thousand students, make new forms of school management imperative. An Alternative Schools Council and District Director of Alternative Schools are newly created agents with increased responsibility for overseeing the alternatives. While both are answerable to the Superintendent of Schools and to the Assistant Superintendent for Instruction, they are given considerable delegated authority and responsibility. The Board of Education has created an Experimental Schools Support Office.

* *Ibid.*, p. 22.

Each alternative has its own director and its local advisory committee, with increasing responsibilities for developing policies. The attempt here is to reverse the traditional "from-the-top-down" flow of decision-making. The alternatives framework is beginning to develop a "from-the-bottom-up" system of school government.

In Berkeley, the Central Board of Education and the Superintendent of Schools have "decentralized" decision-making, and each educational alternative assumes increased voice and accountability for its program. Since each option is available community-wide, the educational consumer has increased opportunities for both participation in and satisfaction with his public schools.

Educational options don't just happen. In the Berkeley approach to alternatives, early experience with Other Ways and Community High triggered a number of basic questions: How—by what process—can viable instructional options be designed? To what extent does liking a teacher—regardless of teaching style—influence a parent's choice of alternatives? What combinations of teacher personality and instructional style contribute to distinctive educational environments?

To approach these and other basic questions sensibly, Berkeley adopted a "phasing strategy" for implementation of its alternatives. The 1970–71 academic year was split into two phases. The first phase provided opportunities for those community residents, teachers, administrators and students who were most attracted to alternatives to volunteer to organize and plan together on instructional options. The second phase provided opportunities to test out a few options, revising them from the experience gained. The Central Administration of the Berkeley district collaborated with these planning teams in the field. For instance, the Central Office provided consultant help to these groups.

It is difficult to anticipate all the problems which are likely to surface in the participatory process of generating educational options. Certainly, if sub-units of a main school are being considered, a range of logistical problems emerges, including the problems of the allocation of human and material resources. However, a sympathetic central school administration working cooperatively with all the interested parties involved in the implementation, will usually be able to overcome developmental problems.

Yet alternatives do not always develop in preconceived fashions. Some are triggered by a group of teachers, others by students, and still others by parents or by a concerned building principal. Perhaps an account of how the Jefferson elementary school embarked on its alternatives program may be useful.

The principal of the school, Mary Georgi, reported that a year prior to her going to Jefferson (she had been principal of a school in the San Roma district), many parents had complained to the superintendent of schools about the lack of an exciting educational environment at the school. This flow of concern continued during Ms. Georgi's first year on her new job. Attempts were made to improve the standard educational program to which all children had to adjust. Ms. Georgi wrote to me in February 1972:

One day, however, one more parent came to see me again asking why there could not be more diversity of educational approaches at Jefferson. (I guess this was the "straw that broke the camel's back!") In utter frustration (having used consultants as catalysts for change and seeing very little), I called the Superintendent's office and asked if I could visit in between appointments to see him briefly. I was fortunate in being able to talk to Dick Foster for a few minutes at which time I said very simply, "I finally know what kind of a school I want. I want a school where parents can choose the kind of education they want for their child and where we can have several forms of education taking place under the umbrella of one school." Dick smiled and said, "Is that all you want?" I replied, "Yes," thanked him for listening and returned to Jefferson, feeling better having expressed my desire but not knowing how it could all become a reality.

This took place about the time the Ford Foundation was considering making a grant to Berkeley. Ms. Georgi's visit to the superintendent resulted in her being given an opportunity to participate in the Ford Foundation proposal. She had ten days to prepare her own proposal. Frantically, and with little input from the staff, she put together a draft. Once the proposal was written, the staff at Jefferson was given released time to consider it. The proposal sought to divide the school into three parts—a traditional school, an individualized-personalized school, a bilingual school.

Ms. Georgi's letter reports the results:

Staff members were given the first opportunity to become a part of the Jefferson Three-Part Model which required a definite commitment on their part. Everyone chose to remain . . . The next step was to inform parents and, of course, many were excited with the opportunity to select the model of their choice. We had four parent meetings with very large attendance, ranging from 450 at one meeting to 175 at the smallest meeting. They took place in May and June. Staff began intensive workshop training in August, prior to the opening of school. There was much excitement on the part of teachers as they had chosen the model in which they most wanted to teach.

The staff at Jefferson had several other meetings with the parents at which there were further attempts to clarify each of the three options. Families were also counseled individually. Other school personnel, for example, the school psychologist, played important roles during this parent-counseling phase.

Then the school sent each family a questionnaire which provided the opportunity to make a choice among the three alternatives. The children were "phased" into their options. In

November, for instance, the kindergarten and first-grade children were placed in the models. In December, the second- and third-grade children were placed.

Once all the children had been assigned to an option, opportunities for transfers were provided. Principal Georgi reports that only six parents asked for transfers—a contrast from the previous year when a hundred and fifty parents had requested transfers. Of the six parents requesting transfers, just one remained dissatisfied—she wanted a "free school," something the principal felt she was not yet ready to mount.

Since then, the Tri-Part School is progressing. Site Advisory Committees have been formed for each model. A Site Advisory Evaluation Committee, composed of staff members and parents, helps in continuous assessment and refinement.

Each of the models continues its communication with parents.

DISTINCTIVENESS OF THE ALTERNATIVES

Each of the more than twenty alternatives developed within the Berkeley Unified School District has its own particular uniqueness.

However, for the purpose of categorizing, the overall distinctive features of the units are here depicted as falling into one of four major areas: *

1. *Multiculture Schools:*—These schools will have children carefully selected on the basis of diversity—racial, socio-economic, age and sex. During part of the school day the students will meet and work together. At other times they will meet in groups related to their own culture to study the language, customs, history and heritage or other special related curriculum.

On occasion these aspects would be shared with the wider groups.

* These descriptions are taken from the "proposals" mentioned above and published as *Alternate Schools,* cited below.

Pupils would learn from the strengths and weaknesses of each group. In a deliberate and planned way they would learn to appreciate differences but at the same time to break down polarization.

One example of the multiculture system is a school called Equal One. Students will be drawn from black, Chicano, Asian and European-American groups. For at least one class period each day the students will be grouped according to their ethnic backgrounds, working with teachers from their own racial backgrounds on studies related to their racial heritage. At other times the students will enter into inter-ethnic group activities and instruction to share, acquaint and inform other groups about ethnic history, literature, music, food and art through programs, displays, parties, reports, etc. Whatever the activity, wherever it occurs, academic skills will be attached to it. The primary objective is to foster instruction leading the students to awareness of their interests, abilities, and capabilities, and to awareness of their uniqueness as well as what they have in common with others.

Another school of this type is Jefferson. A multicultural emphasis is found in each of the three model programs at Jefferson. The multicultural bilingual model uses Spanish and Chinese language and culture as vehicles for gaining insight into and understanding other peoples. In the Individualized Personalized Learning Model students are initiators and parents are included as teachers. The traditional model has come increasingly to emphasize how to reach into the community and to bring into the school representatives of various cultures. All the models will in the future participate in the multicultural activities where they can create, experience and learn about different modes of learning.

2. *Community Schools:* The organization, curriculum and the teaching approach of these schools comes from outside the classroom—from the community. There could be total parent involvement moving both the school day and week into shared family life. Use would be made of courts of law, markets, museums, parks, theaters, and a variety of other educational resources in the community. The schools will be multi-aged and ungraded with an emphasis on real-life problem-solving. Children will work together on projects, with teachers and parents acting more as resource people than as directors of learning. Emphasis would be on learning together rather than through individual competition, and on developing a multicultural community of participating families that learn from each other. There would be opportuni-

ties for the older children to gain work experience through active employment in various community agencies, businesses or projects.

Home and school will be integrated, and learning will take place in the context of problems and projects that are viewed as important by the child and his family. In this multicultural community, use will be made of each person's unique educational resources and competencies. Learning will be organized around the process of problem-solving: planning, trying out, documenting and evaluating. Basic skills would be mastered as need for them arose in the work projects. An apprenticeship prototype would allow for active participation of all ages of students, parents and other community members.

3. *Structured Skills Training Schools*—Schools of this type would emphasize the learning of basic skills—reading, writing and math. Learning would take place primarily in the classroom and would be directed by either one teacher or a team of teachers. Usually the schools would be small subschools within the larger school, affording both teacher and students the opportunity of having close personal relationships, and permitting the use of special facilities, equipment and interdepartmental enrichment. Each of these schools, while offering structured programs, will have distinct personalities due to the thrust of their programs, clientèle, age, interest and need.

4. *Schools Without Walls*—These schools are student-oriented, focusing on child development and the techniques which meet individual student need. The teacher's role will be that of facilitator for learning, of coordinator with parents, of observer in the whole process. The schools will be nongraded, offering fluidity of movement according to student interest and ability in learning situations. The conventional school structure will be modified to facilitate continuous progress for each child, eliminating the necessity of grade standards and social promotion. The goals will be that students grow through self understanding, that they master the basic and social skills through their own interests, and that they become progressively responsible for self-direction in learning and growth.

An example of Schools without Walls is one called Other Ways. Traditionally, students have not had the opportunity to take an active part in shaping their community. Other Ways, started in 1968, provides an "open classroom" antidote to the "system" school for students who are bored or alienated. It provides an educational setting that will encourage a student's participation in his life in a more direct way. In addition to formal courses, there are many informal experiences in living and learning. Special emphasis is placed upon integration of technology into the curriculum, demonstrating that technology need not be denied, but can be used humanely and creatively.*

The diverse sets of educational alternatives are unified by the common set of objectives to which each is addressed. Most educational objectives are written in two ways. The first is a description of general purposes. The second attempts to describe the objectives in behavioral terms, i.e., what the learner is expected actually to do as a result of the program.

Berkeley sets forth both types of objectives. The overriding goals are: †

1. To establish and develop through the process of student, staff and community involvement and participation an educational system that will value and use the innate abilities and individual interests of each child in ways that will challenge, motivate and equip him to be responsible for his own well-being and that of the society in which he lives. (Implicit in this statement is the realization that public education must bear the responsibility for individual and group survival; that education must indeed reflect the needs of the total society.)

2. As a means to meet the diverse needs of all its students and staff, to serve the community more effectively, and to broaden its role in social responsibility and leadership, the District also proposes a series of corollary goals:

    A. To provide a system of Alternate Schools which will consciously and conscientiously work toward the elimination of racism in the schools and the larger community, and will establish measurable programs for the acquisition of basic skills for those youngsters with learning problems, especially those from racial and socio-economic minority groups.

    B. If and when feasible, the Alternate Schools system will depart

---

* *Alternate Schools*, A proposal submitted to the U.S. Office of Education Experimental Schools Program by Berkeley Unified School District, April 6, 1971, pp. 25–28; 58–62.

† *Ibid.*, pp. 28–33.

from the traditional patterns of organizational structure in order to provide a relevant education (i.e., one which has a vital connection to human life) for the students within its system.

C. The Alternate Schools will offer programs and related activities which will provide ways to identify, preserve and promote the cultural pluralisms represented in the larger community, to capitalize on them in an effort to create and foster a viable Berkeley-American culture.

Behavioral objectives are established for each alternative program. For example, one of the behavioral objectives for the John Muir Development Center (see p. 103) is described as follows:

Students in grades K-3 will demonstrate consistent growth in basic skills as measured by standardized tests, with each child who has spent 2 years in the program and completed third grade testing at a minimal proficiency level of grade 4.0. They will demonstrate:
1. growth in creative abilities;
2. increased self-reliance and competence in self-selected learning activities related to learning centers;
3. sustained enthusiasm for learning;
4. increased adaptability in social relationships
as measured by child study techniques, including observation, and parent interviews.*

One of the behavioral objectives of the Berkeley High School-Model A School is reported as follows:

During the school year through reading labs, personalized instruction and group activities will be designed so that students will develop word attack skills that will permit them to decode words at or above grade level. These skills will include such processes as decoding, syllabicating and discerning spelling patterns; the Gray Oral Reading

* *Experimental Schools Program 1971*, U.S. Department of Health, Education and Welfare/Office of Education, U.S. Government Printing Office, 1972, p. 23.

Tests will be evaluated by the district's reading comprehension testing system.*

Obviously, in implementing these alternative schools, there were numerous problems. Berkeley was able to ask the staffs of the various alternative programs, in response to questions from the U.S. Office of Education, about the problems that confronted them. Some of the problems mentioned were:

Lack of inservice training
Lack of cohesiveness in the alternatives structured to serve students
    only part of their time at school
Covert hostility, particularly between those teachers and parents who
    are not a part of alternatives-program and see alternatives as creat-
    ing a drain on the regular program
Directing a multiplicity of programs
Communication problem
Staffs are beginning to realize that they don't have all the answers in
    terms of how to deal with low-achieving students. Many of the sites
    are now really grappling with the problem of how to effectively de-
    liver the basic academic skills to all children
Some of the sites are struggling with the need to determine how much
    discipline and structure is appropriate
Traditional methods of keeping parents and community informed are
    not sufficient . . . creative and new approaches to community aware-
    ness and information are needed
There has been a great deal of redistribution of power among students,
    parents and the wider community. As more actors, representing
    wide diversities, get into the act, the problem develops of dealing
    with a diversity of perspectives; of really listening and really hear-
    ing; of demonstrating that the senders from that plural audience
    have been heard. There are various levels of readiness in defining
    involvement at the decision-making level. Until now, the discourse on
    involvement has been largely rhetoric. Now, with a pluralistic com-
    munity taking involvement as their serious responsibility, the issue
    moves from rhetoric to confrontation. Staff is finding out that
    parents have many different ideas on what true community involve-

* *Ibid.*, p. 35.

ment means. There is a need to help directors and staff learn how to share the decision-making process
In general, those involved in alternative education are learning how painful it all is. And out of that pain will emerge, hopefully, a whole new society of alternatives.*

The Berkeley Alternatives Education Plan is now in high gear. Though changes are still occurring daily, the plan has already received national attention.

Other districts too are considering an alternatives framework. For instance, proposals for alternatives have been developed by the New Haven Public School System, Community School District No. 3 in New York City, and the Quincy Public Schools in Illinois.

While the move toward total system reform through educational pluralism is very much underway in the United States, most public schools are at different stages of development, as examples in the next chapter reveal.

* Berkeley Unified School District Progress Report to the U.S. Office of Education, March 17, 1972, p. 8–9.

V / THE NATIONAL RISE IN
EDUCATIONAL ALTERNATIVES

A fundamental assumption of Public Schools of Choice is that there are always new educational options available, whether in practical form or only as ideas for study and future application. I have suggested that distinctive educational alternatives have indeed always existed, to some extent at least, outside the framework of public education. These have included academic prep schools like Andover, Choate, Mt. Hermon, or Northfield; day schools like Collegiate in New York City, the Commonwealth School in Boston or Horace Mann in New York; religious-affiliated schools like the National Cathedral School in Washington, D.C., St. Paul's in New Hampshire or Germantown Friends in Philadelphia; progressive independent schools like Walden and the Little Red Schoolhouse in New York City, Fieldston in Riverdale, New York; the Montessori Day Schools for preschool children. Now educational options are forming within the public schools at such a rate as to approach a major movement in American education.

Further, on college and university campuses, education departments have been promoting the idea of alternative schools. Three professors at Indiana University, for example, have organized a National Consortium for Options in Public Education to foster the development of alternative schools within public and parochial education. This consortium has members from twenty-five states. The Carnegie Foundation has funded the Center for New Schools in Chicago to assist school districts in developing alternative schools. The University of Massachusetts at Amherst now has an Alternative School Unit designed to explore the concept. This unit describes its role as "joining in partnership with two or three public school districts in the United States to create, implement, and sustain alternatives." Several national periodicals have also emphasized a focus on alternatives in education.*

Thus hundreds of educational alternatives have been developed in the past decade, and the number increases daily. Many of the options have emerged as alternatives *to* the public school. Some have been viewed as parallel schools—standing alongside the public school system, but not part of it—serving students who have been "turned off" by the standard schools in their communities. At times, these alternative schools have demonstrated that the so-called "casualties" (the dropouts and those beyond discipline) of the public school could survive and even flourish in other educational environments. In New York City, for example, the Street Academies and Harlem Prep have embraced disaffected youngsters, and the results have been staggering.

In 1966, with the aid of a Ford Foundation grant, the New

---

* *Changing Schools,* An Occasional Newsletter on Alternate Schools, School of Education, Indiana University; *Alternatives in American Education,* Center for the Study of Education, Arvada, Colorado; *New Schools Exchange,* Santa Barbara, California; *The Worksheet,* Committee of Community Schools, New York City.

York Urban League Street Academies Program launched a program to rehabilitate high school dropouts in ghetto communities. That effort has been incredibly successful in finding, motivating, and training youngsters for careers and higher education. Its high retrieval rate stems at least in part from its employment of trained street workers who are themselves street academy graduates or products of the same background.

. . . They make the first contacts with young people who have left school, helping them get necessary aid from social and antipoverty programs, helping them when necessary in problems with the police, courts, probation agencies. Then they identify among these contacts the large number of young people who have the ability and drive to find a way into productive life through further education.*

The schools function in storefronts and similar locations, and the faculty is comprised largely of street workers. The Street Academy offers a climate of respect, discipline and sophistication —a climate which nurtures the repair of educational deficiencies, and ultimately motivates further education at Harlem and Newark Prep. This program has helped thousands of young people, and is now receiving industry support; more than fifteen firms contribute an average of $15,000 per year. The Street Academy's high rate of success has made it an attractive model, and now Newark, Detroit, San Francisco and Chicago have similar programs. Since the Street Academies are in competition with public school authorities in the cities where they are established, we may hope that they will be incorporated, to some extent, into their local systems. In New York City, for instance, the streetworker component has been incorporated into certain alternative programs such as the mini-school (see page 125).

Alternatives, of course, have not been limited to urban school districts, to minority schools, or to private schools. On the con-

* Thomas E. Cooney, *Report of New York Urban League Street Academies Program*, April 14, 1970.

trary, today's movement toward alternatives is essentially a middle class, public school venture. Alternative programs are being offered or planned in such affluent districts as Great Neck, N.Y., and Newton, Mass. And alternatives have not only appeared as separate institutions, but often as diverse classroom settings within a single school. In order to clarify the full range of educational alternatives, it is useful to describe the various types that exist.

CLASSROOM ALTERNATIVES

Classroom Alternatives function at the *individual classroom level*. Teachers have styles of teaching which lend support to either a standard or open (informal) classroom environment. Many teachers feel constricted by the uniformity of public schools, and are searching for alternatives which may be more compatible with their own professional personalities. Some teachers are learning "Montessori" methods, others "behavior modification" techniques.

At the present time, the concept of the "open classroom" is very fashionable. Colleges and universities are involved in all sorts of activities designed to explore its possibilities. Adopting any *one* alternative, however, regardless of its appeal, comes into conflict with the challenge of human diversity and undermines the concept of education as the fulcrum of a democratic society. The open or informal classroom is significant, not because it ought necessarily to replace the standard classroom but because it is a valid *alternative* for many teachers, students, and parents for whom the standard form has ceased to function.

THE "OPEN" CLASSROOM ALTERNATIVE

In recent years, informal classrooms have sprung up from coast to coast; "informal," "open," "British Infant," "integrated-day school," "child-centered" are all, for our purposes, synonymous terms for one view of education—a view which has its early roots in American "progressive education," and which has been refined in Leicestershire, England, since the second World War. Much of our current informal education can be traced directly to the "progressive education" period in American education (pre-World War II) and to the massive influence of philosopher John Dewey), but more should, perhaps, be attributed to the modern British Infant School.

The term "integrated-day" refers to a classroom in which the academic disciplines are synthesized ("integrated") on the basis of the interests, concerns, and experiences of the learner. For example, children interested in cooking may decide to bake a cake. In the process of baking the cake, the children learn new words, must read recipes, must learn different measurements, etc. These basic skills are integrated around a common experience.

Thousands of American educators visit England every year to observe the British informal classrooms at firsthand. In this country, nearly every state has encouraged some form of informal education. The State Commissioner of Education in New York State has endorsed the concept, and has designated funds to foster its implementation. North Dakota is earning a national reputation as a leader in the informal, child-centered approach. Through the efforts of the University of North Dakota's New School for Behavioral Studies in Education, hundreds of teachers are being trained and retrained in the open classroom method.

It is not clear to what extent the recently developed open classrooms are the result of student and parent choice. There are some indications that these classrooms are being implemented because teachers, rather than parents, consider them more desirable. Nonetheless, we repeat our point that any alternative which is imposed on the public is not really an alternative at all.

The following memorandum, sent by the State-supported Campus School of the State University College at New Paltz,

New York, is an example of an administration encouraging parental decision-making in the choice between "open" and "traditional" classrooms:

To help you in considering the optional programs, we will try to describe the essential differences.

The Standard Program

In the standard classroom, the skill areas and academic content have an obvious structure which is largely teacher designed. This is achieved within a prescribed daily schedule in which subject areas tend to be discrete. The child in the course of each day receives specific assignments and is designated certain responsibilities by the teacher, which may be carried out individually or in small groups, in order that he develop knowledge, attitudes and skills to cope with the adult model of society which he is entering.

The standard classroom tends to be self-contained, maintaining the usual desks and other accepted furnishings and physical arrangements of the typical classroom. Opportunities for free exploration are usually limited to specific time blocks.

The Open Program

The teacher prepares a rich and stimulating environment in which each child is allowed to make decisions regarding his selection and pursuit of curricular activities, the time he spends on various content areas, and the manner in which he goes about learning. All areas of curriculum are integrated within the child's choices.

The teacher's responsibility is to guide the child to achieve balance in his choice of learning experiences while helping him develop knowledge, attitudes, and skills to cope with the immediate and larger societies in which he lives.

The visual image of the open school is one of intense, purposeful activity both inside and outside the specific classroom. Interest centers for exploration, experimentation, problem solving and creativity make the open classroom a workshop in the truest sense.*

---

* Communication to parents, State University College, Campus School, New Paltz, New York, 1971.

SCHOOLS WITHIN SCHOOLS

Another emerging pattern for providing educational alternatives is "schools-within-schools." Under this organizational plan, one elementary or secondary school is transformed into multiple "schools"—that is, one school offering a uniform program for everyone is converted into two or more schools within the same building, each offering a different sort of educational format. For instance, schools-within-schools can offer the student a choice of standard, open, or multiculture framework.

Schools-within-schools are attractive for the parent, student, or teacher who prefers neighborhood education. But the process of converting to a schools-within-schools approach presents administrative complications, and any institution considering the prospect would do well to examine previous attempts. We offer some examples:

Walt Whitman High School is in Bethesda, Maryland, an affluent suburb of Washington, D.C. Not long ago, a group of students, supported by the faculty, developed a proposal for a schools-within-the-school plan. Walt Whitman was reorganized on the premise that a pluralistic school community requires pluralistic programs and methods in its educational system. With this notion in mind, small schools were set up within the larger school to enable teachers and students to work closely with one another, spending their time with more flexibility. With about 125 to 150 students and a team of five teachers, each of these schools functions as a group for most of the school day. The teacher teams establish programs of study that have been agreed upon in cooperation with their participating students.

The schools are organized to suit the various educational needs and interests of both students and teachers. Some of the schools are typically traditional and highly structured. Other schools are considerably less structured, with youngsters and faculty members outlining and executing programs jointly. Thus, the schools are set up according to teacher-and-learner philosophy. A few of the schools, however, are designed around broad content areas: Ecology—Natural and Human; Urban Studies; History and the Arts; Science, Technology and Culture; the Counter Culture; Fine Arts Workshop; Existentialism—Philosophy and Psychology; Human Relations; Foreign Cultures and Languages; Modern Technology; American Studies; Comparative Religion; Utopian Thought.* These subject areas are not the equivalent of majors, but act as central themes which embrace several areas of study.

It was proposed ". . . that schools could be organized by both content and philosophy, e.g. one Urban Studies School could be unstructured, giving students and teachers equal responsibility for planning, while another could be highly structured, with a thoroughly teacher-planned and teacher-executed program. Organized this way, the many needs of students and teachers could be met." †

Not only do the schools vary in their educational philosophies and curricular activities, but school hours, meeting places, and regulations also differ. The "schools" all meet at Walt Whitman and in other settings, not necessarily within conventional school hours. Since no two schools are exactly the same, attendance policies, scheduling methods, and other regulations differ from school to school. Schools may exist for a semester, a year, or for any time block considered appropriate.

Here the schools-within-schools approach has established sets of options for students and teachers, and within them the two

* This list is taken from proposals drawn up by the students of Walt Whitman High School, 1970.
† Ibid.

groups have been able to find a school that is both comfortable and satisfying.

Haaren High School in New York City provided the model for the setting of the Hollywood movie *Up the Down Staircase*. Today the school would be a less appropriate target for criticism —it has been re-organized into "mini-schools" or "schools-within-a-school." In an effort to encourage closer relationships between teachers and students and to alleviate the burdens of bureaucracy, the school organization was dismantled and re-structured in the form of semiautonomous "mini-schools." Each has 150 students, half a dozen teachers, a course adviser, and a street worker.

Each mini-school functions around a common theme, e.g., "urban affairs," "creative arts," "aviation." In addition, students in all the mini-schools pursue a nuclear curriculum of English, social studies, and mathematics. The school consists of a cluster of classrooms with an informal student-teacher lounge at its center. Each mini-school occupies its own area of the six-story, sixty-eight-year-old building overlooking the Hudson River. For the most part, students and teachers spend the entire school-day in the section of the building assigned to the group. The primary aim of Haaren's internal decentralization is to convert each mini-school into an equivalent of the sixteen small, informal "alternative" high schools that have been established as off-shoots of the eighteen regular high schools throughout the city.

Hostility and distrust between students and teachers is reportedly disappearing in the atmosphere of the casual, face-to-face contact that has developed in some of these "alternative" schools, for example, in Manhattan's Harambee Prep, a satellite of Haaren and Hughes High Schools, and in Brooklyn's Wingate Prep.

But these small alternative schools, although they are offering models to the educational public, involve only a minuscule proportion of the students of the parent schools. The Haaren venture, on the other hand, represents the Board of Education's one and only attempt at wholesale, top-to-bottom restructuring of an entire public high school. Because it is not the typical hothouse experiment of teacher volunteers and student guinea pigs, the project is considered highly significant. If it does succeed in improving an institution as troubled as Haaren used to be, the supporters of the mini-school concept contend, this method can dramatically change any high school for the better.*

The public school system of Newton, Massachusetts, has always been regarded as one of the finest in the country. Recently, Newton High School instituted its Murray Road Annex. The Murray Road School is an alternative within the public school framework. Technically, it is not a separate school, but an annex to Newton High School.

In 1967, Newton High School was overcrowded, and the Murray Road Elementary School was offered to it as a way of easing the pressure. Since the schools were not close to each other, it was recommended that Murray Road operate independently, and that it experiment with new ideas that might be useful in the programming and design of new high schools. The experiment focused on two particular ideas: ". . . that students could take a great deal more responsibility for their own education, and that teachers and students could collaborate on the establishment and development of curriculum." †

Ronald Gross and Paul Osterman, in their book, *High School*, portray Murray Road as a place where:

. . . students do not have to be there unless they actually have a scheduled class or want to be there to use the facilities or to meet their friends. There is no set curriculum. What "curriculum" there is is de-

* "Troubled Haaren Tries the Minischool," in *The New York Times*, November 17, 1971, page 49.

† Evans Clinchy, "Murray Road: Beyond Innovation," in *High School* by Ronald Gross and Paul Osterman. Simon and Schuster, 1971, p. 241.

vised collaboratively by the students and teachers. There are no grades. There is no principal. (The teachers elect one of their number to handle the administrative chores on a rotating basis.)

The atmosphere of the school could hardly be less formal. The halls are filled with students and teachers moving entirely on their own, going about their business. There is no such thing as a "pass" to go anywhere inside or outside the building. Classes are held in classrooms, in the hall, out on the lawn under trees, depending upon how people feel at the moment (and upon the weather). Classes are also held at night in homes, if they cannot be squeezed into the schedule. (The school is supposed to be closed at 4:30 every afternoon.) *

Like so many other schools, Murray Road School's physical facilities are hopelessly uninspired. The institution was built in the fifties, and it consists of "eight largish rooms. Some are typical, 1,000 square-foot, elementary school classrooms." The larger rooms are used as "A) a commons room, equipped with a refrigerator, battered old chairs, and a ping-pong table (the school's one piece of physical education equipment), or B) an art studio equipped not so much for teaching as for students doing their own art projects." †

Murray Road, because it does not have a cafeteria (students bring their own lunches), science labs, language labs, guidance units (or guidance counselors), a football team, cheerleaders, industrial arts, or home economics facilities, is a fairly inexpensive school to operate, and can easily afford its 14 to 1 pupil-teacher ratio. As Gross and Osterman point out, expenses are low because "much of the operating is done by the students themselves. After the teachers and students have together decided what the 'courses' will be for the coming semester, the schedule is worked out by a committee of three students."

Disciplinary problems at Murray Road are minimal, and the general tendency is toward cooperation:

* *Ibid.*, p. 237.
† *Ibid.*, p. 236.

. . . the teachers and the students collaborate on all of the important decisions. Since there are virtually no rules, it is difficult to have discipline problems. There are two major requirements—every student must take something called "English" and, at some point, a year of something labeled "American History" (this is a state law). Seventy-five minutes a week of "physical education" is also required. But this is done on the honor system. Otherwise, students make suggestions about what they would like to study—computer programming, astrology, the origins of man, child psychology, etc. The teachers set forth what they would like to teach—logic, linear algebra, the alienated individual in literature, comparative myths, French conversation, etc. The final catalogue is made up of the compromises worked out by students and teachers. Teachers, however, decide how many "credit hours" any particular course is eligible for. All students must end up with a total of sixty-five credits for their three high school years, the number of credits required for all Newton High School students. At the end of a course, the teacher and student evaluate the student's performance. Usually, the student and teacher will agree on whether credit has been earned, but if there is any disagreement, the teacher's judgment prevails.

If students cannot find a teacher to teach what they want, they are free to set up and "teach" their own course. They can receive credit if a teacher evaluates their work and pronounces it fit.*

The San Diego City Schools has a school-within-a-school in its William Howard Taft Junior High School. Under the sympathetic leadership of principal Edward B. Anderson, a group of teachers planned the Taft Interdisciplinary School (TIS). Initiated in the spring of 1970, Taft Interdisciplinary School is physically located at Taft Junior High, but operates as a subunit of the school. The teachers who pioneered this concept describe their reasons:

Several facts of school life have encouraged this departure. Primarily, teachers do not work closely enough to really get to know their students. While one teacher may have only 160 students a day, he can seldom, if ever, find a colleague who has the same students. Effective

* *Op. cit.*, pp. 237–8.

teaching, especially if one wishes to individualize, requires a solid understanding of the student. Secondly, as students go from teacher to teacher, they are subjected to a variety of philosophies and attitudes. It is possible for a relatively small number of teachers to accept a common philosophy about learning and practice it as they are continually in communication. Thirdly, teachers want to be accountable professionals; they have from time to time expressed a desire to run their own school. This will be both an opportunity and a challenge to these adventurers.*

Thus, nine teachers who believed that an alternative to a compartmentalized by subject or discipline (e.g., math, English, social studies, etc.) approach to learning should be available to students agreed to start a school within a school. Their concept for this alternative was an interdisciplinary and united approach to teaching and learning.

Administratively the TIS relies on staff cooperation. As an integral part of Taft Junior High, TIS is responsible to the principal of the school.

There are 300 students in TIS and ten teachers. The remainder of Taft Junior High has 1,300 students.

The TIS staff offers instruction in all the areas normally taught. Some students who desire to take courses not offered by TIS take them at the regular Junior High. Mini-courses which have been offered by TIS teachers include:

Wars of the World	Economics
Ecology	African History
Urban Studies	Criminology
Indians	Anthropology
Social Problems	Sociology
Political Problems	Local Government
Juvenile Delinquency	Minorities
Psychology	Debate
Social Simulations	Shakespeare

* Unpublished mimeographed statement, "Taft Interdisciplinary School —1970–1971."

At Quincy High School II, a school-within-a-school plan is called "Education by Choice." This effort serves about 1,500 students and involves eighty teachers in the eleventh and twelfth grades of District 172, Quincy, Adams County, Illinois.

After a comprehensive period of planning, a program developed which is described as follows:

Education by Choice

After giving much consideration to the individual differences of students and teachers, Quincy Senior High II (for juniors and seniors) has developed a program designed to maximize the educational opportunities for students. The program, called *Education by Choice*, will offer to students a series of different learning environments called alternative schools.

Each alternative school will be composed of small groups of teachers and students and will be designed to provide different approaches to learning. While all smaller schools will be seeking similiar academic and personal goals, the learning activities and methods of instruction will differ, thereby providing several routes for students to attain common educational goals.

This program has been in the planning stage for over a year as a result of a grant from Title III, E.S.E.A., a federally funded project. It has been developed by secondary teachers through many workshops and planning meetings. Finally, it was felt that this program should be implemented for juniors and seniors. Teachers have submitted a further proposal to Title III, E.S.E.A. in hopes of receiving an additional grant to help initiate the new idea.

The result of all the planning is that seven alternative schools are being presented to students of Senior High II for 1973–74. Students, with assistance from parents, counselors, and teachers, will choose one of the alternative schools. Every effort will be made to match each student's learning style, interest and self-discipline with a school which offers him the greatest potential for educational and personal growth. Each small school will offer English and social studies and as many other fields as possible with the teachers in that particular school. In some cases, students will take subjects in one of the schools which is outside his choice. For example, there is only one German teacher so students will have to go to the school in which he teaches.

Why have we developed "Education By Choice" in Quincy? The sixties in education will probably be recorded in the history of education as the "innovative years." Many programs to individualize education have made their way on the nation's educational scene. Our P.I.E. program is one of these. The impact has been so great that education may never be the same again, regardless of what finally happens. This individualized instruction generally means the right of every individual to acquire an education within the school system in his own way and at his own rate of learning. Many innovative schools have emerged to implement a program of individualization but, for various reasons, many of these have reached a plateau and leveled off, or have retrenched. We, in Quincy, believe we can profit from the errors which accompanied massive innovations in the sixties and continue individualization in a more reasonable and effective pattern.

Quincy Senior High II, then, will be one of the leaders in developing alternative schools. We feel our staff of teachers has shown the commitment, flexibility, and ability to make each smaller school an important choice for students.

The following sections will give the reader more information about each of the alternative schools proposed for 1973–74. They are:

A. Traditional (typifies education in the past)

B. Flexible (utilizes a flexible modular schedule)

C. P.I.E. (individualized approach)

D. Fine Arts (focus on art, music, drama, and humanities)

E. Work-Study (special program now in operation)

F. Special Education (special program now in operation)

H. Career (associated with new vocational school) *

SEPARATE ALTERNATIVE SCHOOLS

Another prominent approach to Public Schools of Choice is to develop full alternative institutions. Under this plan parents, teachers, and students all agree to start a separate public school. The outstanding definitive quality here is that the participating

* From a pamphlet entitled *Education by Choice, Title III, E.S.E.A., Alternative Schools in Quincy Senior II.*

parties are involved in creating a *separate* structure—usually an alternative school within the existing public system.

Separate alternative public schools do have distinct advantages. They do not have to infringe on the culture of an established school. It is clear that any school operating for any length of time will develop its own unique social system, with its peculiar set of acceptable patterns. This is an argument often raised *against* schools-within-schools and *for* separate alternative schools.

The St. Paul Open School in Minnesota is an alternative school which acts as a research and demonstration unit of the St. Paul Public School System. Joe Norton, one of the participants in the school, describes it thus:

I am writing to tell you about a school in which you might be interested—the St. Paul Open School. 13 months ago a group of parents and kids came together to get an alternative within the St. Paul Public School System. The group, calling itself "Alternatives, Inc." grew to over 2000 people and was successful in convincing the Board of Education to attempt the idea if outside funding could be obtained. Grants from Title III and the Hill Family Foundation were received—and we opened 2 months ago in a former warehouse.

We have 500 students, ages 5–18, who voluntarily come to the school from all areas of St. Paul. The 500 represent all ethnic, minority and income groups of the city. St. Paul's minority school-age population is approximately 10%—our school's is between 12–14% and hopefully will increase.

We have different areas within the school building, as well as internships, apprenticeships and multidisciplinary trips. Each student chooses his or her own advisor, with whom a weekly schedule is planned. The student makes the final decision. NO activity is required, other than respect for others in the community. Kids, staff and parents planned the inside of the building—until late August it was a Univac warehouse. Together we decided on what to put where, which partitions to tear down and which to leave up—and even what colors (red, orange, purple, black, green, blue, etc.) to paint walls, doors, etc. The school is in a constant state of change!

I am one of the very lucky people who were offered an opportunity to do things with kids in this situation. I help plan trips (such as one to the Badlands and Pine Ridge Reservation in South Dakota, planned with the American Indian Movement so kids really learned about life on reservations, and one to Gettysburg this spring with a group who want to find out about the Civil War and its effect on them). I also help kids get into apprenticeships and internships, help them learn about Nonviolence as a Means of Change, 3rd World Revolutionary Movements, Young People and the Law, history of contacts between whites and Indians, and projects to help improve the environment in which we live (ranging from a 7-year-old's neighborhood cleanup to some teenagers trying to organize their neighborhood to get enough pressure on a business to eliminate the smell—and work with the Pollution Control Agency to get stronger anti-smell laws). . . .*

The school is organized into major learning areas, or "theatres of learning": music-drama, humanities, math-science, industrial arts, home economics, and physical education. Each area has a library-resource center. Many areas have rooms for quiet study, short courses, and group or individual projects. A weekly schedule reveals a host of ongoing courses, from a 9:00 A.M. course in Talking About Our Dreams to one in Russian at 3:00 P.M.

When a student is not involved in one of the activities going on at all times, he may be meeting with his adviser. Together, they continue to chart the student's goals and determine the appropriate means of achieving them. When a given project or course of action doesn't fulfill its expectations, the goals are revised or the methods are altered. The student explores his own strengths and weaknesses, his talents and handicaps, and eventually, he comes to know the limits of his intellect and his social behavior. Students determine their individual schedules, learn to design their own educational programs, and thus build a structure of self-initiation.

* From a letter written to the author November 13, 1971.

This approach integrates the various disciplines. Basic skills are incorporated into the broader learning situations, and teachers determine appropriate ways to interweave them. In the case of a film project, for example, "Students read manuals, photo magazines, and books on the subject, keep logs or rearrange demonstrations, purchase materials, determine proportions and ratios for enlargements, and thus constantly use and become familiar with reading, writing and math, at whatever level they're operating." *

The staff and students feel mistakes are a necessary and useful part of learning. Learning at the open school is conceived not only in terms of mastering cognitive skills, but also in terms of developing the less definable, but equally important qualities needed in a rapidly changing society: flexibility, openness, initiative, curiosity, enthusiasm.

Teachers (or "learning facilitators," as they prefer to be called) "spend their energy and thought on maximizing learning for students." They are assisted by aides, volunteers, student teachers, and various resource people. But, more than any others, they are assisted by the students themselves—"who, by the very nature of the entire enterprise, are in natural roles of teachers-and-learners."

Older students serve as models for the younger students by providing leadership and teaching. This responsibility role counteracts the sense of impotence among many teenagers, and enables them to direct their great energy into creative channels. Younger children benefit by more individual attention and personal help from those who are in a sympathetic position. And the young children help the even younger children.

Teachers were selected for the faculty of the St. Paul Open School on the basis of three criteria: interest, competence, and educational philosophy—"a distinct advantage over reassigning

* From the brochure, *The St. Paul Open School* by Wayne Jennings, Director.

or retraining a traditional staff." The teachers themselves are democratically organized and make decisions on additional personnel, training, budgetary changes—"thus increasing their understanding of these decisions and their feeling of responsibility toward making them work." Students and parents are invited to participate in the frequent faculty meetings. When staff members lack the know-how to handle a specific situation or task, they explore possible solutions together "through training sessions or more informal means." They work closely with parents and interested citizens, as well as students, on an elected advisory council.

One of the goals of this project is to demonstrate that, given sufficient equipment and materials, learning can take place even with a limited professional staff. The money saved on teacher salaries can and should be put into the "stuff" of learning.*

A student at the St. Paul Open School describes what the "stuff" of learning is for him:

This is my second year at the Open School. In this short time, many, many, wonderful things have happened to me. One of the things I enjoy most is the open and friendly atmosphere. This may be due to minimizing competition and stressing cooperation. There is no pressure to get A's or worry about tests because there are no grades. Since the school is more concerned with learning than attire, we don't have to worry about the length of our hair or the "right" kind of clothes. There are no required classes at the school, so rather than taking wood shop, which I dislike, I use that time to take biology or photography. I much prefer learning about the structure of the heart to building a pipe rack. My classes are varied and are geared to be taken at my own speed. That way, if I don't understand a concept, I can spend more time on it. There are few, if any, age restrictions, so if I want to take an advanced math class, I can.

Since our school enrolls students from ages five to eighteen, I go to classes with kids of all ages and we help teach each other as well as learning from the teacher. If there's a class that I want and it isn't

* *Ibid.*

offered, I can initiate it myself. There's always someone around to help out. I take a few independent courses where I'm my own teacher. I set goals, and, in most cases, accomplish them. Most classes I take are those I'm interested in, although there are a few classes I don't like much but need to take for my future plans, so I attend them, too. Some of my classes are: biology, chemistry, geometry, reading, writing, photography, news analysis, contemporary society, video taping, and driver's education. . . .*

In Great Neck, New York, where over 90 percent of the high school students go on to college, the search for alternatives triggered the establishment of the Village School. This high school was opened in the 1970–71 term. A group of forty-eight high school students and three teachers helped forge this alternative. Chosen from a list of two hundred students who applied, the students of the Village School are free to attend seminars in such subjects as modern politics, political philosophy, ethnic relations, Shakespeare, comparative literature, Latin American mythology, logic, statistics, computers.

Students are also free not to attend courses. They can plan other activities on their own. For instance, some students are enrolled in adult programs in the evenings. Others are taking courses at Adelphi College. Individual students may serve as interns in various community agencies. One student was an intern at *Newsday*. Independent study is also a component for most students at Village School.

In a special edition of the Great Neck Public Schools *Newsletter*, the value of the Village School was noted:

It's not the wide range of learning activities, however, that makes the Village School so unique to its students. What seems to have far greater meaning is the freedom to devote their time and energies to what most concerns them. And since different concerns crop up at different times, demanding new changes on the schedule board, they meet

* From *Changing Schools*, An Occasional Newsletter on Alternative Schools, No. 005, p. 3.

together at least once a week to agree on which "disposable structures" they might try on next.

... students are finding colleges willing to accept their Village School experience in lieu of more traditional high school courses. Some nearby colleges like Queens and Adelphi even send teams of student teachers to the school for training. One group of apprentice teachers recently arrived from as far away as Bethany College in West Virginia.*

The Needham Public School System in Needham, Massachusetts, is also involved in an innovative program of alternative public schools. The following is an abstract of the statement on the alternative high school:

That alternative high school program will provide up to one hundred students the opportunity to develop their own learning experiences in a democratic fashion. With the aid of three regular teachers, as well as interns and community resources, students will chart their own educational course within the basic framework of requirements established by the State Department of Education and Needham School Committee.

The Alternative Program Community will be housed in two rooms at the High School where required tutorial and general meetings will be held.

The success of this program will be gauged and its implications for other programs in the Needham Public Schools will be considered through a series of evaluative reports.

Operationally, the alternative program functions under the auspices of the Needham School Committee, and conforms to the requirements established for high school education by the Massachusetts Board of Education and the Needham School Committee.

A. All students entering their junior or senior years of high school are eligible for the program. Special exceptions may be made by the Needham High School Principal.

* 1970–71 Midyear Edition of the Great Neck Public Schools *Newsletter*, p. 2.

B. Students will submit an application, including a statement of parental approval, by a date set by the Principal.

C. If more than the hundred students provided for apply, the selection process will be done by random computer sampling weighted to achieve a balance of juniors and seniors, male and female.

Students are expected to maintain acceptable academic and behavioral standards as determined by the staff and students of the program. Failure to do so may mean separation from the program. In addition, they must comply with the following requirements:

a. Students must attend a weekly general meeting of the staff and student body to discuss problems, determine policy, decide on disciplinary matters, attendance, management, and other procedures.

b. Each student must attend a weekly tutorial group meeting for at least two hours. This group shall be limited to fifteen randomly selected students. The meetings, led by one AHS teacher and at least one college intern, if available, may include group activities and discussions or may split into individual conferences between teacher and student. The main purpose of this group is to provide:

(1) An opportunity for an adviser to get to know a student as an individual, to determine his needs, and to help direct him toward goal fulfillment.

(2) A chance to evaluate the progress of the alternative program and to work toward the solution of problems.

(3) A group relations experience where the student is expected to learn to work effectively with a group he did not choose.

c. Students, in consultation, may propose learning experiences that may result in either individual projects or course offerings.

d. Prior to the development of an individual program, an estimate of credits shall be made.

e. Credits for existing courses at Needham High School shall serve as a guide in determining credits.

IF THIS PROGRAM DOES SUCCEED ACCORDING TO THE CRITERIA OF AN EVALUATIVE STUDY, THE POSSIBLE IMPLICATIONS FOR THE STUDENTS WOULD INCLUDE:

a. A sense of personal pride in being part of a successful, innovative program.

b. A feeling of need fulfillment—the attainment of at least some of the objectives stated in the guidelines.
c. An increased ability to achieve (or the achievement of) a large measure of self-direction and motivation.
d. For seniors—a feeling of adequate preparation for their chosen goals.
e. For juniors—a chance to continue in the program through graduation.

AND THE IMPLICATIONS FOR THE PROGRAM WOULD BE:

a. That preplanning and changes which occurred throughout the year were well-advised.
b. That the program be continued as is or expanded for a larger number of students (possibly including sophomores) and teachers.
c. Possibility may exist for allocation of more funds on the basis of success.
d. Procedural or structural changes will be made in the guidelines based on the year's experiences. The program should not become unresponsive to new ideas just because of one year of success.

Tulsa, Oklahoma, has developed several alternative schools within its public school system, and one of them is Project 12. This Project was launched in August, 1970, under the funding of the Youth Opportunity Service in the Office of Economic Opportunity. During that first year, the Project worked with approximately 170 students.

Although the curriculum resembles that of the traditional high school, it does have distinct differences. One is its heavy emphasis on "practical" needs, i.e., Family Planning, Career Exploration, Income Management, and the improvement of self-image. Instruction tends to be more innovative and individualized than traditional public school teaching. Community consultants and "field" learning situations are stressed to insure an overall flexible approach toward teaching and learning. One unusual aspect is that Project 12 estimates an expenditure of $450.00 per student, considerably lower than the district's per pupil cost. The structure within Project 12 is totally nongraded, with students of ages fourteen to twenty-six working together in small groups or individually.

Students are able to enroll in the project on the simple basis of available space. Preference is given to individuals who demonstrate an unusual, immediate need to be in the school. These may be students who are referred to the project by a community agency or court official. The student body is diverse, bound by a common failure in the conventional high school setting.

Each failure has its own story which might involve one or any combination of several factors:

These [the factors involved in failure] include family responsibilities and problems, personality conflicts, academic failures, legal entanglements or just a strong dislike for school in general. Some students who have been out of school for two or so years may simply refuse to return to a regular school, either because being older makes them feel uncomfortable or because they cannot "tolerate" the time necessary for graduation or both.

The students not only have diverse cultural and social backgrounds, but also vary in ability. Contrary to popular belief, dropouts are not necessarily "slow" students. Enrollment thus far has shown a student range from *remedial* to *accelerated*. Students vary in ambition and attitude as well. For some, high school graduation is a matter of pride. As the Tulsa Public School brochure states,

. . . among this group is a housewife who simply wants to prove to herself she can "do it." Others view graduation as a necessary step leading to some type of college training. Still others need a diploma as an immediate means of getting a particular job. And, of course, there are those without any specific aim who simply realize the basic value of education.*

* All materials regarding the Tulsa Public Schools are taken from the brochure *Tulsa Public Schools—Alternative Schools.*

Pioneer High School, a public school in Ann Arbor, Michigan, has proposed the creation of Pioneer Two, another experiment in Alternative Education. Pioneer Two, based on a self-generated request on the part of approximately sixty high school students and members of the faculty, is geared so that students can learn from one another. Like a School Without Walls, the learning environment is greatly expanded, and a learning-centered education is provided which allows the student to work according to his own abilities. Students attending the school receive full academic credit; the curriculum is determined through various discussion groups by the students themselves.

The program of Pioneer Two is a reflection of the community, faculty, and students. At present, the school consists of one hundred students, chosen on a voluntary and random basis from the applying population of Pioneer High School. It is staffed in part by the teachers of Pioneer High School, and in part by community resource people.*

The Molalla, Oregon, School District, populated largely by poor white youngsters, has begun to develop some innovative school programs. Molalla has the highest concentration of welfare families in the state of Oregon. Moreover, many families have moved into the district with children who have histories of educational difficulties. Most of the developed programs have been aimed at the high school level. Of the three thousand students, it is estimated that eight hundred would benefit greatly by programs other than the traditional model.

Molalla's special program was developed originally for thirty seniors who had been disaffected in their past school experiences. There is, according to state law, only one classroom course requirement and that is something called "Modern Problems." Two teachers are assigned these students, and they see that this re-

---

* "Students Plan Curriculum in Pioneer II 'Orientation,'" in the *Ann Arbor News*, Ann Arbor, Michigan, Wednesday, October 13, 1971.

quirement is met. For the remainder of the school day, each youngster, with the guidance of his sponsoring teacher, develops a schedule of his own. "Students may spend the day either within the school or out in the community. During the school year each student must have the following experiences: 1) work, 2) service, 3) teaching, and 4) exchange." * Youngsters with problems in a particular subject area at the high school level may receive full credit by tutoring students at the grade school level in the same subject. One hundred sixty students participated in this program in 1971–72.

Under the sponsorship of one teacher, twenty-four boys are released for one-half of the regular school day to construct an $18,000 home. For this, the youngsters receive Math, English, and Construction credit. Many other youngsters are involved indirectly in the related aspects of bookkeeping, design, landscaping, etc.

Students are permitted to take courses at the local community college, and high school credit is given for this.

An interdisciplinary approach to learning is often effective, and ninety freshmen are involved in one such program, which includes vocational survey, math, and English. Here a vocational subject has been used as a springboard for teaching math and English.†

The Pacoima Elementary school in Los Angeles has revamped its structure, with the assistance of the System Developmental Corporation, as a community-oriented institution where children teach each other. The Tutorial Community Project (TCP) is a seven-year effort to establish a model school based on the creative use of human resources. In TCP everyone learns from everyone else.‡

---

* All materials on the Molalla Schools are taken from a brochure published by the Molalla, Oregon, School District.

† *Ibid.*

‡ Tutorial Community Project Progress Report, July 19, 1972, by Gerald

... Since the project began in September, 1968, the S.D.C. has focused on reorganizing the kindergarten classes and planning for changes in the first grade. Fifth and sixth grade students have been trained to tutor the kindergarten children in a range of subjects including story-telling, art, writing, learning the alphabet, reading, and numbers. The results have been encouraging. The older children—responding to the challenge—performed intelligently in their assignments; the younger children learned faster and better. Even students with behavior problems improved after becoming tutors. Teachers have had more time to teach on a one-to-one basis.

In addition, the school established new ties with the community and with parents through teacher-parent meetings, home visits, and "encounter groups," where grievances are aired and barriers to change are confronted.

The Los Angeles Board of Education, which endorses and participates in the project, says it has "already demonstrated potential significance in improved achievement by disadvantaged children." *

In September 1971, the project expanded to include two more elementary schools, Wilshire Crest and Dublin Avenue.

The Mamaroneck Public School System, in a suburb of New York City, proposed and prepared a high school (E.S. 70) to operate as an industrial corporation. This program, a simulation of a corporate system within the school, reflects the nature of the industrial world—a world which absorbs the bulk of our work-force. It examines industrial and technological influences, and their effects on our culture and people. The school corporation actually designs, manufactures, and markets products.

This integrated practical arts program has thus far satisfied Mamaroneck's expectations for E.S. 70. It has helped create an environment in which individuals learn to act cooperatively to achieve common goals. Within this framework, individualizing means that students examine and select the work areas best

Newmark, taken from *News from the Ford Foundation*, April 28, 1970, by Richard Magat and Whitman Bassow.
 * *Ibid.*

suited to their abilities and study them to the fullest possible extent. As an established alternative to the Mamaroneck High School, E.S. 70 is thus providing choices.*

Recently, Metropolitan Denver has instituted two programs for undermotivated potential high school dropouts in the Cherry Creek High School "I" Project. The Project, a Title III ESEA program, is located in a cottagelike building four and a half miles from the Cherry Creek High School campus. There is also a program located on the campus for the ninth and tenth grade students who seem ill-suited to the nuclear high school.

In the ninth and tenth grade program, one is apt to find students sitting on the floor studying. A relaxed atmosphere prevails at the cottage and at the on-campus setting; there is a soft drink machine, rock music, and an extremely casual teacher-student manner. There is no such thing as a typical day. "It [the program] is open to change or flexibility of scheduling, to more kids' taking part in an hour-long discussion about society problems or the novel they are reading than in a regular course of study in social studies or the English novel." †

Generally, student's schedules revolve around laboratory courses in basic skills built on diagnosis, prescription, and assessment framework. Pre- and post-tests are administered to evaluate the student's proficiencies at the close of each nine-week period. The idea is to accept the student at his own level. At the same time, there are short-term—six- or nine-week—classes based on student interest; these are designed to motivate students to build on their strengths, and to remediate their weaknesses.

The kids, once termed "undermotivated" students, can now be seen tackling the problems of setting up a company to sell the objects they have made themselves.

---

* From the brochure *Mamaroneck Industrial Corporation Project*, distributed by the Practical Arts Department, Mamaroneck Schools, p. 3.

† From the brochure: *Cherry Creek I Project*, October 26, 1971.

The cottage program has a small staff: three teachers and two interns. The eleventh and twelfth grade students at the cottage spend the morning in academic courses, and the afternoon at jobs or in related work activities. Students are given credit for consistent work and retention of jobs. Students are integrated into other classes on the campus when they indicate the appropriate interest or ability. Prevocational concepts are introduced—how to get a job, how to keep a job; and students are learning about the world of work in detail. The focus here, as in many alternative programs, is on the student himself.

Established several years ago, the Multi-Culture Institute in San Francisco, a private day school for children from three to nine years old, emphasizes racial and ethnic differences among its students. The San Francisco institute divides the entire curriculum and every school day into two separate components. One is totally integrated: the other is deliberately segregated, ethnically and racially.

In the morning, all children work together in fully integrated classes in such lessons as reading, English and mathematics. In the afternoon, each ethnic group meets in its own separate class, with each class under a teacher of the same background and skilled in the particular group's cultural heritage.

For example, the Jewish group would study Hebrew; the black group Swahili; the Chinese group, Mandarin or Cantonese; the Spanish-Americans, Spanish. Similarly, each group would deal with the arts, crafts, and culture of its heritage. Each plans dramatic and musical programs, particularly in preparation for its special holidays, and each studies and cooks the foods of its own tradition.

The separatist part of the day is never conducted as a means of encouraging ethnic or racial isolation or supremacy. When the children have prepared their own national food, or are ready to present their plays or to celebrate their holidays, all the others are invited to join, to compare, and to learn.

The meaning of a Jewish Passover, celebrating liberation from oppression, thus becomes a meaningful counterpart of the black children's celebrations of civil rights milestones.

The rest of the children—those who do not fit into the category of what are presently considered ethnic or minority groups—spend their afternoons in a "poly-ethnic group." There, they too explore their several cultural pasts, although with less intensity and with a view to comprehending a variety of cultures.

The multi-ethnic approach stresses the fact that the United States is —except for the Indians—a nation of immigrants and that everybody belongs to an ethnic group. The old concept of Americanization through the public schools calls for a suppression of the minorities' ethnic traditions, often even at the risk of a severe cultural break between parents and children. The multi-ethnic doctrine aims at sharing of the more general aspects of American life and ideals, but without submerging the ethnic, racial, and religious heritage of the different groups.*

Those who advocate this new concept stress "that the old melting pot approach has created not only angry resistance on the part of the last-arrived minorities, but also a sense of rootlessness among the children of the old established groups." This original multiculture school has helped many public schools plan similar programs.

City schools are the most in need of educational alternatives, and Philadelphia has pioneered in this field with the Parkway project—the School Without Walls:

The Parkway Program is an experimental high school that has no building of its own, but uses all of downtown Philadelphia as an educational resource. Instead of sitting in classrooms memorizing textbooks, Parkway students learn through direct experience in hospitals, universities, theaters, offices, and the large number of cultural institutions—among them the Musem of Art, the Franklin Institute, and the Free Library—that line the Benjamin Franklin Parkway, an elegant boulevard stretching from City Hall to the art museum a mile away.†

* "How to Be Very Different Yet Still Get Along," in *The New York Times*, Sunday, April 11, 1971.

† Henry Resnik, "Parkway: A School Without Walls," in *High School* edited by Ronald Gross and Paul Osterman, New York, Simon and Schuster, Inc., 1971, p. 249.

A Parkway student's day may include a course in journalism at the Philadelphia *Bulletin*, taught by the newspaper's staff, a lecture in physical science at the Franklin Institute, lunch at a convenient restaurant, a tutorial in the art museum. (A group of eighteen or so is the unit, something like a family, in which students receive counseling, instruction in basic skills, and evaluation, in the afternoon.

The curriculum in the Parkway Program allows the student to explore his interests, and to learn and develop his talents. What is emphasized is the student's growth in the context of the school and the surrounding city. Within broad state requirements for high school accreditation, he can study just about anything he wants—eighteen courses in the Parkway catalogue, for example, fulfill the state math requirements.

Course offerings include some taught by the program's own staff, ranging from basic skills to activities like yoga. Also included are courses taught by people other than the staff; these cover a spectrum from on-the-job training in local businesses to demonstration lectures at various institutions. There are three separate units in the program (Alpha, Beta, Gamma), each with its own headquarters and catalogue; each catalogue lists roughly 90 courses from which students can choose.

"High Schools Without Walls," following the Philadelphia pattern, have now been launched in other places. For instance, the New Haven Public Schools has a "High School in the Community," the Hartford Public Schools a similar school it calls "Shanti."

The New York City Schools has a school without walls that has been described in the following manner:

A "City as School" opened in September 1972 with 100 students. Various "activity and learning" units included companies, institutes and agencies such as IBM, the Legal Aid Society, Brooklyn Museum and Brooklyn Academy of Arts and Sciences. Fifteen high school students joined with school administrators in the planning.

In November 1971 New York City opened the Downtown Academies with 32 students. Fifteen months later the enrollment was up to 240 volunteer students in the program, which combines academic studies with on-the-job training in nearby offices or large corporations. The academies provide alternative weeks of study and on-the-job training, with the students paid for the work. Companies agree to hire graduates for full-time employment.*

The school district of Philadelphia has developed still other options:

Education has to do with learning, not schooling. It is a process which takes place in a community as people come together to learn from one another. Formal curricula violate this principle whenever they become inflexible, disintegrated, or insensitive to the uniqueness, excellence and integrity of each individual involved.†

The school district of Philadelphia has come through a long and difficult struggle in order to understand and to act upon this principle.

A year after Parkway was in operation, the Chicago Board of Education established a similar experiment. The Chicago Public High School for Metropolitan Studies (Metro to the students) was a school without walls in the Chicago Public Schools. At Metro, classes meet at various business and cultural institutions in the city. About 350 students are enrolled, although the demand is in the thousands. This program, like Parkway, attempts to expand the learning environment for its students.

. . . Metro began with the belief that the best way to acquaint the student with the real world is to dissolve the walls separating the student from the city by integrating the world into the student's daily cur-

* From *Alternative Schools: Pioneering Districts Create Options for Students*, publication of the National School Public Relations Association, 1972, p. 17.

† Except as otherwise noted, all materials on the Philadelphia public schools come from the brochure of the School District of Philadelphia.

riculum. If a student wants to learn about aquatic life, the school should develop a class taught by a professional marine biologist at the city's aquarium. If another is interested in economics, a class should be created at a bank or a brokerage house. This basic philosophy allows the student to know that there is a wealth of knowledge to be obtained through countless resources in the city which surrounds the school. The student then must be helped to learn how to tap that knowledge and make it work for him. To implement this philosophy Metro has developed a program which offers an extensive variety of academic experiences.

Among the courses offered at Metro are Principles of Economics, Advanced Fundamentals of Writing, Nazi Germany, Animal and Human Behavior, T.V. Production, Math Lab, the History of Western Art, Art and Community, and many others.

Also, Metro students can initiate their own independent study projects with teachers. They can also take classes at the city colleges.*

The Beloit-Turner Middle School in Wisconsin is experimenting with the unique interests, needs, and goals of sixth, seventh and eighth graders.

The visitor's first impression of the school is one of openness—of wide-open, visually attractive space. His second impression is one of almost constant movement, relatively quiet, purposeful, and relaxed, but unceasing. Only later in the day does he realize that he has heard no bells ringing to signal the end of class periods, and that classes of various sizes have met for differing lengths of time, and then have dissolved and reformed with a minimum of disturbance.†

The school is the result of a community effort to find a better way of meeting the educational needs of early adolescents. No

* From a mimeographed leaflet describing the Philosophy and Academic Programs of Metro.

† Maurice Hillson and Ronald T. Hyman, editors, *Change and Innovation in Elementary and Secondary Education*, Holt, Rinehart and Winston, Inc., 1971.

federal, state or foundation funds were involved. The program, through the efforts of teachers and students, has been kept as flexible as possible.

. . . the day is divided into three large blocks of broad objectives. One half of the day is allotted to "Developing Social Sensitivity and Understanding" (which draws on the social studies, English, and foreign languages), one quarter of the day to the "Physical Environment" (which focuses on science and math), and the remainder of the day to "Developing Creative Interests and Abilities" (which offers students freedom to develop their own interests in art, music, home economics, and industrial arts). Each large group of students works with a team of teachers, teaching assistants, and interns, as well as with specialists. The instructional program itself is not predetermined, but is relegated to on-the-spot, day-by-day, week-by-week planning of the teaching team and the students. The part of the day devoted to the creative arts leaves the student free to choose his own area of interest—and to change it at will.*

The program is still evolving, as with other alternatives that we have mentioned; its eventual success will depend on the participation of those involved—parents, teachers, and students.

The school system of Gary, Indiana, was the nation's first major school system to contract with a private education service company. They chose the Behavioral Research Laboratory (BRL) to operate one of their elementary schools (Banneker), on a money-back guarantee performance basis. Banneker has been transformed into a nongraded center where students attend courses in five curriculum areas: language arts, mathematics, social studies, science, and enrichment.

In 1970, Dr. Alfonso D. Holiday, President of the School Board, announced his reasons for initiating the project: "The basic educational reason for this contract is the gross underachievement of our children. We are at rock-bottom and must

* Ibid.

try new approaches to educate our children. We must be willing to be pioneers, and no longer say our children can't learn."

While this particular contract school was dropped by the Gary Board of Education at the beginning of 1973, the experiment did reveal some valuable features. For example, the educational goal of Banneker was to provide every learner with the opportunity to achieve the level of his potential, and the tactic was across-the-board individualization. The individualized system allowed the child to work at a level he could handle, to move ahead when he had acquired the necessary skills, and to receive professional attention whenever he needed it.

. . . They [BRL] have prepared instructional objectives for the entire math and language arts program.

They have created a number of learning activities in which the learner can engage to accomplish any one objective.

They have done away with "grade levels" because they do not adequately represent each learner's progress in the instructional program.

They have developed "pre-tests" for every unit of the math and language arts programs.

They have developed a system whereby certified personnel prescribe activities for each learner in language arts and math.

They made it possible for the certified person to circulate around the learning area and interact with each learner on the learning activity in which he is engaged.

They have a system whereby the certified person can prescribe new learning activities on the spot to overcome specific problems.

They provide many points at which the learner's progress is measured.

All personnel receive training in the principles and techniques of social reinforcement.

To maintain this individualized system, support systems were developed to make the appropriate instructional opportunities available for each learner. Among these support systems were:

A) training and in-service programs for teachers, para-professionals and administrators;

B) flexible scheduling models to enable learners to transfer between learning levels;

C) procedures to ensure that appropriate materials and resources are made available to the learner when he is ready for them;
D) an enrichment laboratory to which learners may be assigned for short periods to receive special assistance in areas which need remediation.*

The attitude of the public toward education has been impressive in the Broward County Public School System in Florida. Parents have been deeply concerned with the development of a better educational program for their children. Business and industrial leaders have, to a surprising degree, been aware that a superior school system is the backbone of a growing community. The leadership of educators, the willingness of the public to accept new ideas, and the need for vastly improved public school programs have produced the Nova High School, an exciting experiment in instructional reform in this progressive community.

Nova's primary purpose has been to utilize scientific methods of learning, with an educational program truly tailored to individual needs. Nova has put into practice the theory of "taking each student as far as he can go." Motivation on an individual level is nurtured by Nova's nongraded method of progression. As a student masters each of a series of achievement levels in a course, he goes on to the next level. No one can fail, and no one is required to repeat a full year's work in any subject. Students progress through the school's program at their own rate, and they depart from the basic program of studies according to individual interest and ability.

Eliminating grades is only one part of Nova High School's fresh concept of meaningful education. Operating on a trimester system, Nova has lengthened its school day and year. The daily schedule includes five regular class periods, each seventy minutes long, plus an optional period for research or participation in

* From the brochure of the Banneker Contracted Curriculum Center, Gary, Indiana, 1970.

noncredit, cocurricular activities. The school year here is 200 days long—forty days longer than the national average, and forty days longer than the Florida law requirement.

Nova High School has a cross-section of youngsters, for it refuses to concentrate on the "gifted." It was obvious from the first that this novel approach to education held considerable promise for the students, and teachers expressed equal enthusiasm for the plan.

Perhaps the most intriguing aspect of the program is the natural, nongraded progression. Parents are particularly pleased with the prospect of their children's being challenged on a constant basis. All agree that each student at Nova High School is motivated to do his very best, and, again, the focal point of the institution has been shifted to the learner.

The curriculum is presented to the student in the form of a study unit, a general plan serving the function of a text, study contract, curriculum guide, lesson plan, and resource reference. Any given unit must clearly outline the nature of areas to be studied, exhibit a discernible continuity, issue a challenge to the student's interest (regardless how remote that interest might seem to be), and still take into account differences in individual ability. Thus, within each study unit, various projects can be accomplished by youngsters with disparate objectives.

In the midst of all these individual differences, Nova emphasizes a "hard-core" curriculum. All students must take English, mathematics, science, a foreign language, social science, technical science, and physical education during every school year.

At first, students were grouped on the basis of their records from previous schools. Further testing and evaluation during the school year resulted in adjustments, and students are now grouped according to achievement. Learning situations are organized to meet specific needs. Methods range from large-group instruction—with teaching teams and guest lecturers—to regular classroom instruction, seminar discussion in small clusters, and individual research. Talented students who demonstrate rapid progress may graduate early with the approval of the faculty. However, no one is graduated in less than two and one-third years beyond the ninth grade. Nova's purpose is not to graduate students early, but to give them a broader and deeper education over a longer period of time.

COMPREHENSIVE, DISTRICTWIDE ALTERNATIVES

In a previous chapter, we described Berkeley's districtwide approach to educational alternatives. Other public school districts also are working on more comprehensive alternative education proposals.

The goal of the Philadelphia School District is to create a climate that fosters creativity, freedom of expression, and a desire for learning. It is the ideal of the District that educational experience be exciting and enjoyable, and that it be related to the real needs of people as they try to understand and cope with the world in which they live. The District also holds that education, if it is to satisfy an entire community of learners, must cut across such boundaries as age, sex, color, and status.

To achieve these goals several settings have been established as learning environments in Philadelphia:

A. *The Durham Learning Center* where teachers, parents and students experience learning as a total-environment process. The center is a model of continuous, coordinated, comprehensive services and education for children from infancy to age ten. Other learning centers operate in schools throughout the district.
B. *The Early Childhood Follow Through* models (with over five thousand students): the Education Development Center; Bank Street; Florida Parent Educator; Behavioral Analysis; Bilingual–Bicultural; Local Parent Implemented; and the Philadelphia Process Approach.
C. *The Intensive Learning Center* which provides an alternative educational process for elementary school children based on individual

need. In addition, it assists participating elementary schools in implementing programs that have demonstrated improved pupil performance in basic skills.

D. *The Affective Education Program* which considers how a child feels in relation to how he thinks. The program emphasizes a "process approach" to learning. It operates in more than forty-five schools and influences over eight thousand students from levels 1–12.

E. *The Conwell Middle School* with a computerized sequencing and scheduling program which provides students with flexibility, diversity and increased range of educational opportunity.

F. *The Pickett Community School,* a pilot middle school model of intensive community participation and community-school integration.

G. *The Pennsylvania Advancement School* which has attacked the concept of "underachiever" at the middle school level with personalized attention and instruction.

These programs have proved successful in providing free and dynamic environments for group learning, and have supplied the Philadelphia School District with a cadre of educators who are skilled in developing and managing innovation.

The School District of Philadelphia has a Director of Alternative Programs who is coordinating the development of forty-six proposed alternate learning environments. These are reported to be modeled "after open classrooms, schools without walls, mini-schools, schools for students with special problems (gifted learners, academic failures, disruptive pupils, pregnant students . . .)"

The Minneapolis Public Schools have initiated a Southeast Alternatives Program serving all students in that area of the city. Any elementary student can attend any of the following four types of schools:

1. A contemporary school, Tuttle, which offers curriculum innovations, but maintains a teacher-directed, structured curriculum and grade-level school organization.

2. A continuous progress school, a part of Pratt and Motley schools, in which each child advances at his own pace without regard to grade level and in which instruction is team-taught and based on a carefully sequenced curriculum in basic skills.

3. An open school, Marcy, which combines flexible curriculum, scheduling and age grouping in the style of the British infant schools. Children take a great deal of initiative for their own education with the emphasis on pursuing their own interests.
4. A free school, named the Minneapolis Free School, which extends through the 12th-grade level. Students, parents, volunteers and faculty develop the courses, and much off-campus experience is included. The initial enrollment of 70 students will be expanded to 150 during 1972–73 and a more structured, content-oriented program will be developed, according to school officials.*

In March 1973, the Minneapolis School Board voted unanimously to adopt a policy extending the program of alternative education on a districtwide basis.

The Alum Rock Schools in California are participating in a voucher experiment. Parents in this pilot project receive vouchers worth about $680 for children in elementary school and abcut $970 for those in the seventh and eighth grade. Six schools and about 4,000 students are involved. Each of the six schools offers at least two alternative programs. If the evaluation of the initial years proves positive, then the demonstration will expand during the subsequent years.†

OTHER PROPOSED ALTERNATIVES

In the previous section, various types of alternatives are described which either already exist or are being considered by public school systems across the United States. It is by no means a complete list, but it gives the reader an idea of the extent to which new forms of education are being developed. This section is devoted to a sketching of two more proposed alternatives,

---

* *Alternate Schools*, a publication of the National School Public Relations Association, p. 23.

† The Alum Rock experiment is described more fully in Chapter VII.

which may or may not come to fruition. They can give you an idea of the "endless" possibilities for creating new kinds of schools.

The Wildwood School, a preschool fostering awareness of nature and man's place in nature, is being planned in Aspen, Colorado. Its advocates believe that the public schools have fallen far behind in innovating programs to deal with environmental problems, and they propose the school be situated so that:

. . . it is hard to tell where the natural learning environment ends and the school environment begins. Wildwood blends so well with the landscape that it is almost unrecognizable from a short distance.

The organic form of architecture enables us to incorporate many natural features dear to a child's heart. What child wouldn't want to follow an otter down a slippery slide, walk behind a waterfall, or observe fish and ducks in the pond through an underwater viewing window? How many children could resist the opportunity to slide down a rabbit hole to enter their classroom?

There is an aura surrounding Wildwood which recalls the magic of fairy tales and other children's stories, such as *Alice's Adventures in Wonderland, Winnie the Pooh,* and *The Wind in the Willows.* The scale of the building, its form and setting insure an intimate relationship between the child and his "sense of place" for learning and play.*

Not only is the setting of the school unique and exciting; the school's approach to learning is just as exciting in its use of nature as an inspiration:

Nature and art are the twin foci of the Wildwood School program and they coexist under unique conditions. Most schools teach natural history, expecting uncreative return of the same information, then move on to art and treat it as a completely different subject. Wildwood, however, departs from existing educational methodology. We like to think of the educational process as a continuous input–output feedback

* *The Wildwood School,* from a brochure by Robert B. Lewis and Associates, of the Educational Research Group, Aspen, Colorado, 1971.

loop, whereby *nature* and *art* are constantly influencing and reinforcing each other. For example, if one of the inputs of the morning's activities is centered around the frog, the afternoon's activities might revolve around representation of the frog through one of the art media. To help him more fully understand and personally identify with the frog, a child might also choose to project a cartridge film loop, listen to a tape of frog choruses, or listen to a story read by the teacher about frogs.*

In *Making Urban Schools Work,*† Gerald Weinstein and I proposed an alternative school to serve as a model for urban schools. We visualize this school as having three distinct areas of responsibility, each assembling appropriate talent and facilities for the tier's set of objectives:

Tier I. Skills and knowledge development
Tier II. Personal talent and interest-identification and development
Tier III. Social action and explorations of self and others

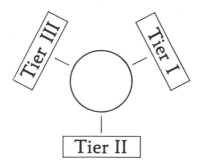

The Three-Tiered School ‡

* *Ibid.*

† Mario Fantini and Gerald Weinstein, *Making Urban Schools Work: Realities and the Urban School.* Holt, Rinehart & Winston, Inc., 1968.

‡ The three-tiered model was suggested to us by Bruce Joyce in the publication *Restructuring Elementary Education: A Multiple Learnings System Approach.* New York: Teachers College, Columbia Univ., 1966, p. 4.

Tier I comprises the objectives related to basic skills, learning-to-learn skills,* information, and the major concepts of specific disciplines that are most needed as essential building.

It is concerned with the development of reading, computation, writing, and speaking skills. It involves also the basic information and ideas contained in the social studies, the natural sciences, and other disciplines appropriate to the learner's stage of development. Also included here would be elements of psychology, sociology, anthropology, and political science—a simplification of the more sophisticated notions that are currently taught in social studies curricula. It is important to note that any substitution here should be weighed with specific reference to the ultimate aim of the school. For example, when considering the study of foreign languages, would it not be of more immediate urgency to offer courses in Spanish, Chinese, Russian or an African dialect, than in the classical Latin or French or German?

It is Tier I that provides the information- and skills-retrieval base. It is the most highly automated, individually paced, self-instructional, materials-centered stratum of education. Most of

* The phrase "learning-to-learn skills" refers to those processes, ways of thinking, examining, or behaving which help the child become more adept at learning. These skills have been described by many educators as: critical thinking, analytic procedures, discussion procedures, rational processes, inquiry, evaluating, problem solving, hypothesizing, planning, predicting outcomes, generating alternatives, classification, analogy, comparison, inductive and deductive reasoning, etc. The point here, however, is that we do not regard these process-skills as an outcome, an end product, in themselves. Although such skills may be handled more or less in a rudimentary way in Tier I, it is in Tiers II and III that we hope they will be exercised to the fullest. For instance, many people believe that if a child can be instructed in critical thinking, that is all he needs. Important as critical thinking and other process-skills are for the learner, we feel that they should be a means, an instrumentality, for helping children work out problems that they are concerned about intrinsically. Thus, while introduced in Tier I, process-skills will be utilized more meaningfully in Tiers II and III.

the current discussion of individualized and programmed instruction is applicable to this tier. Although concentrated attention to Tier I may not exactly spark the imagination, it is efficiency at this level which allows for greater possibilities in Tiers II and III.

Although Tier II is also highly individualized, it has a different texture. In Tier I, content is essentially fed to the child; in Tier II, in contrast, it is elicited from him. It is here that everything from learning to play the tuba to working on a self-designed research project, producing a movie, writing a play, mastering Swahili, occurs.

Tier II embraces also the development of those talents which are usually referred to as "vocational." Marvin Feldman, former Program Officer at the Ford Foundation, offers several points which we feel are pertinent to an emphasis on vocational educational education:

> No effort should be spared to develop appreciation and respect for the varying talents of the individual on the part of the pupil as well as of the school system. A major objective of elementary school education should be to seek out the talent in each and show its relationship to the world of work. . . . [The school should] attempt to acquaint the student with the workings of industry and commerce, and help him match his talents to his career objective. It [also should] include an annual career-objective analysis for each student as diagnosed, discussed, predicted, and evaluated by the combined resources of man-made examinations, computer-oriented methodologies, and man- and machine-derived interpretations.*

Tier III can be understood as a group inquiry into the social issues which relate to the lives of the students, and as exploration of one's self and others. Another level of learning-to-learn skills—"self-and-other awaring skills"—would also be explored in this tier. These are sensitivity skills; they include anything which helps develop a greater range of intensity and effective-

---

* Marvin Feldman, *Making Education Relevant*, Ford Foundation pamphlet, 1966.

ness in expressing emotion to one's self and to others. All too often, these skills are ignored in the traditional classroom; often, when a group of youngsters is asked how they feel about something, they automatically offer a response that they suppose the teacher will agree with or, at least, sanction. The whole business of sensory perception is explored in the third tier.

In Tier III the teacher, by establishing a developmental sequence of awaring skills, can help the children elaborate self and others. Such a developmental sequence might be stated this way:

Skills that facilitate—

Stage 1. Seeing and describing what is happening to you, especially in feeling or behavior states.

Stage 2. Understanding others as they see and describe what is happening to them.

Stage 3. Comparing, contrasting your feeling and behavior responses with those of people around you.

Stage 4. Analyzing the various responses and their consequences.

Stage 5. Testing alternatives—seeing how you feel when experimenting with new feelings and behaviors (for example, trying out the feelings and behaviors of others).

Stage 6. Decision-making, choice-making, from feelings and behaviors you have tested out.

Tier III, thus, would mainly be involved with power, identity, and connectedness, and would allow for a greater emphasis on the affective aspects of education.

VI / LEGITIMIZING OF PUBLIC
SCHOOLS OF CHOICE

LEGITIMIZING EDUCATIONAL ALTERNATIVES

How does an educational alternative become legitimized? What are the bases on which public school officials approve an alternative? How are alternatives initiated and implemented? What are the problems? How are other alternatives doing? Are there theoretical justifications underlying alternatives? We have discussed legitimization by applying the "ground rules" for a Public School of Choice System (pp. 41–54). In addition to these basic principles of understanding, it may be necessary to be more specific. After all, there are state education laws which must be followed. Further, we have made the case for *Public* Schools of Choice, in part, because we feel that the consumer needs to be protected from poor quality and "fraud." Obviously public schools have had to follow state regulations in order to maintain their status. True, the private school too has had to adhere to certain minimal standards to obtain a state charter as

163

a "school." Sometimes *public* school officials serve as evaluators of private, independent schools seeking a state charter.

One possibility for any school or school district contemplating an educational alternatives approach is to establish a set of common criteria based on state education requirements as a guide to the development of educational options. *These criteria are not meant to discourage options—rather they are to serve as common minimal standards.* We have been suggesting that there are different educational paths to common educational ends. Establishing state requirements as minimal standards gives the participants a sense of protection.

The problem of legitimizing options cannot be solved here. Different communities will work out their own patterns. Public schools have a strong element of public accountability attached to them. They are common, nonsectarian institutions. They are responsible for offering opportunities for diverse consumers. As public institutions elementary and secondary schools have responsibility for such objectives as career education and citizenship preparation. These cannot be left to chance. Educational alternatives within public institutions need to recognize these realities.

It would be inappropriate to legitimize educational alternatives which deny the learner opportunities to develop his talents for a career in the real world of work. Unless a student is independently wealthy, he will have to earn a living. Public schools cannot deny a learner an education that will enable him to do so.

As we have already pointed out, if educational alternatives emphasize freedom or happiness at the expense of other goals—say, reading and writing—then it is conceivable that the learner, exposed to such alternatives, may indeed enjoy his schooling, but find himself in the end unable to read or write.

If such were the case, these learners would, once their schooling was completed, find that they were unprepared for any career in the work world. Such an offering cannot be legitimized in a Public School of Choice framework. To do so would be to deny the learner "options" as an adult. However, legitimizing educational alternatives also means dealing with a host of other problems.

ALTERNATIVES BY CHOICE, NOT IMPOSITION

Our experiences with the civil rights freedom schools, the counterculture free schools, and the British open classroom have provided evidence that there are other ways of educating than the pattern found in public schools.

However, while these surfaced as alternatives in education, they were not necessarily based on consumer choice. They usually became alternatives to public schools and outside of their jurisdiction. Whatever the form an alternative took, it was usually accepted by those dissatisfied with public schools—a mere handful in comparison to the large numbers who could be affected within public schools. For those who tried to introduce alternatives within the public schools, the problem was different. Open classrooms, for example, were developed by teachers and were often imposed on the students and parents, on the grounds that this form of education was better than the standard. While many parents and students responded to this alternative, a significant number did not, and they questioned their forced participation.

Further, proponents of many alternatives, in order to establish their legitimacy, waged a fierce attack on the established educational offerings. In short, they made the standard school look bad by comparison. This naturally made those who were content with the standard—professionals and laymen alike—upset and resistive. A political tug-of-war developed which fragmented educational communities and disturbed the instructional climate for both camps.

MAKING ALTERNATIVES ATTRACTIVE
TO THE MAINSTREAM

Moreover, because alternatives had emerged from a background of specialized needs like overcrowded schools or nonadjusting students, i.e., since alternative forms of education were necessary to help children who were having problems, the entire initial public conception of alternative education was cast in an atypical light.

To complicate the situation, some minority communities resisted alternatives because they were different from the normal forms of education. The resentment was expressed by such remarks as, "Why are you giving us something different? Aren't we normal like others? We want what the whites have—not something different." In short, those accepting an alternative would be admitting that something was wrong with them—a verdict already rendered by white society. Moreover, a mood of fiscal austerity vis-à-vis rising school expenditures gripped the mainstream and the public policy makers, including school boards. The natural question became, "Will alternatives cost more money?"

When alternatives were first introduced to the mainstream, the bulk of the samples came from urban settings with minority children or with the counterculture folk. For the mainstream, there were preconceived images of both groupings. Educational programs for blacks are seldom perceived as models for whites. The attitude is almost the same with those programs for "long-haired hippie-type" youth. The first response of the mainstream to alternatives was a resounding "If this is what you're calling alternatives, fine for them but not for us."

However, since the need for alternatives cut across social class lines, it soon penetrated the most prestigiously perceived school systems—the ones looked up to by the mainstream. When descriptions of alternative education come from such school districts as Newton (Massachusetts), Scarsdale and Great Neck (New York), Webster Groves (Missouri)—and when alternative schools are linked with successful college entry—then the mainstream is more likely to respond. The mainstream, the majority who use public schools, need to feel that alternative forms of education do not compromise their sense of equality. Unless an alternative school can give assurance that the student will be equipped for further learning, will succeed in college, the option is doomed.

PSYCHOLOGY OF LABELING

Yet another hindrance to legitimizing alternatives is that those who embrace these alternative forms of education have been too quick to use labels. For instance, when a group proposing an option refers to it as "open," "individualized," or "humanistic," then those in the standard program rightfully respond: "When you use the terms "open," "individualized," "humanistic," are you implying that what we do is closed, non-individualized, dehumanistic? Obviously, our programs are also open, individualized, and humanistic, but we resent the implication."

The psychology of labeling may seem like a minor point in the legitimization process, but it can result in bitter conflict extending beyond semantic differences. Since most of the mainstream are products of the standard alternative, they know it best and tend to feel more secure with it. Proposed alternatives that appear dramatically different are often viewed with extreme caution. Certain conceptions of open education, where students are given considerable freedom, may be viewed as overly permissive and chaotic. Further, mainstream parents will reject alternatives that do not convince them that the educational objectives they have come to value are being emphasized. Thus, even when the open classroom is initially appealing to parents they may soon lose their enthusiasm if children do not bring home schoolbooks and homework (symbols of academic legitimacy to parents who have gone through public schools) or if the basic skills, including reading, are not handled in the structured ways that parents have come to expect.

PARENT EDUCATION

Those who are connected with alternatives sometimes not only lose sight of the importance of parent and public education, but expect parents to learn the whole thing after a few hours of exposure. It is difficult for mainstream parents to accept a child-development point of view that explains that their child will eventually learn to read—perhaps as an adolescent, or whenever he is most ready. Most parents have been oriented to a normal-abnormal view of child growth and development. They are eager to know how well their child is doing vis-à-vis other children his age. They want their child to progress according to age, not by some theoretical notion of development. After all, argue these parents, aren't most schools age-graded?

Mainstream parents may have various motives for considering alternatives, some of which cannot be sanctioned under a public school framework. When the notion of alternatives and choice are packaged together, some may want to use this plan as a way of maintaining or reattaining racial or socioeconomic exclusivity. Why can't an alternative be for all white or all black students? The answer, of course, is that public school alternatives cannot be used to circumvent the law. The concept of alternatives within the framework of public schools involves enhancing the comprehensive goals of human growth. They are tied to the noblest ideals of a free society. Deliberate exclusivity cannot be condoned and is a criterion for determining whether a public school alternative is legitimate.

LACK OF EVALUATION AND STAFF RETOOLING

The Director of the Experimental Schools Program, Robert Binswanger, who has helped support a number of alternative schools, identified several problems in a speech on the subject in San Francisco on February 1, 1973.

Dr. Binswanger emphasized that several alternatives were literally being carved by the blood and sweat of one or two people. He suggested that the round-the-clock effort of a few dedicated persons could not be long sustained. Too often the alternatives fold when the energies of the initiators are dissipated.

The other concern expressed focused on the need for better evaluations of alternative efforts. Binswanger felt that those engaged in alternative education are so busy trying to get them started and developed that they often neglect evaluation.

Another problem raised at regional or national conferences on alternatives has to do with retooling staff. It is clear that many teachers and administrators who are willing to explore other ways of educating learners need retraining. They have the motivation but not the skills. Consequently, staff development opportunities have priority. This need becomes apparent when one considers the "turn away" demand for workshops, institutes and conferences on alternative education, new schools, open education, etc., that have sprung up in the past few years. Increasingly, both school districts and teacher-preparation institutions are trying to mount in-service programs that respond to this growing problem.

In certain school districts where alternatives are being considered, intra-school problems arise over plans that limit the alternatives to a separate school, i.e., if separate schools are favored over schools within schools. In one district, teachers in neighborhood schools opposed a separate alternative school on the grounds that they were left out. They wanted each neighborhood school to develop its own alternatives plan. In this case, supporters of alternative education were divided, not on their commitment to alternatives, but on what strategy was to be employed for implementation.

In some places, the alternatives that are planned increase the per pupil cost. Obviously, skepticism sets in when options are introduced that add costs to budgets already straining. When optional education is presented at the same or slightly lower per student cost, then school district leaders are more likely to be sympathetic.

ALTERNATIVE SCHOOLS REPORT THEIR PROBLEMS

Certain pioneer school districts have begun to show their problems with alternative education even after a short period of involvement with them.

The Seattle Public Schools have about 80,000 students. This district has many of the same educational problems faced by most other schools. Over the past several years a number of alternative schools have "sprung up." Generally these alternatives were of two varieties—dropout prevention and open or innovative.

There are presently thirteen separate alternatives in full time operation and 23 part-time re-entry programs.*

In the summer of 1971, the Superintendent of Schools estab-

* From *Changing Schools*, An Occasional Newsletter on Alternative Schools, No. 003, p. 3.

lished The Alternative Education Task Force to study ways of improving alternative programs in the district. After about a year of study, the Task Force concluded that

(1) the dichotomy between "traditional" or "regular" education and alternative education is a false one; (2) the present "regular" education system, in the Seattle Public Schools, is an initial step in the development of a series of alternatives; and (3) the crucial problem is one of insuring that both "regular" programs and alternative education programs learn and gain self-renewal from mutual commitment to and involvement with one another.*

Among the items reported were the weaknesses of the alternatives program:

... Most of the problem areas enumerated in alternative education indicate a weakness in the organization and structure of alternative education within the District. Common problems included these:
1. Some programs were unable to recognize specific issues and occurrences as symptoms of problems that needed solutions.
2. Some programs were unwilling to define major issues and to ask for support and help before they developed into insoluble problems.
3. Some programs were unwilling to define their staff and programmatic limitations. In other words, at times they tended to "bite off more than they could chew."
4. A few programs had an attitude of "having their cake and eating it too." Some programs wanted ultimate freedom from District control and at the same time, unquestioned support from District resources.
5. In some cases programs did not define strategies and priorities and were often caught in situations which used valuable time but were not significant.
6. Many program managers and head teachers were unable to exert themselves in their roles of leadership and direction.
7. Several programs had entrance criteria which encouraged students to drop out of school and did not allow the program to address itself to the needs of severely alienated students already out of school.

* From *Alternative Education '72*, Report of the Seattle Alternative Education Task Force, p. 30.

8. Some programs demonstrated a lack of awareness of the need to encourage and maintain acceptance and tolerance by the community in which they were located." *

The Task Force concluded its report by supporting alternative education, stating:

. . . If the development of alternatives in education is a viable goal—and it is the contention of this Task Force that it is—then the long-range direction must be toward the convergence of all efforts into a system based on choice. This can happen within the system of public education.†

Problems are important for any group considering alternative education. Since the momentum for optional education can be led by administrator, teacher, parent, student, and the like, it is crucial for all parties of interest to analyze their own situation in terms of the problems identified in the field.

IMPLEMENTING ALTERNATIVE SCHOOLS

We mentioned earlier that our experience this far has revealed that alternatives can be triggered by almost any group. For example, at the Second National Conference on Educational Alternatives at Wingspread in Racine, Wisconsin (1973), this wide range in the parties initiating alternatives was identified:

1. *Administrators Initiate Alternatives:* The Seattle, Washington, Public Schools; the Grand Rapids, Michigan, Public Schools; and the Louisville, Kentucky, Public Schools were among school systems identified where energetic administrators took the lead in developing educational alternatives.
2. *Teachers Initiate Alternatives:* Teachers in the Racine, Wisconsin, Public Schools originated the idea for an alternative school and

* *Ibid.,* pp. 9–10.
† *Ibid.,* p. 23.

worked to sell their board of education and community the value of such an educational approach.

3. *Parents Initiate Alternatives:* In St. Paul, Minnesota, it was a group of concerned parents who petitioned the school board to diversify their educational program by creating an Open School for public school students.

4. *Students Initiate Alternatives:* It was primarily the moving force of students in Newton, Massachusetts, that led to the creation of a public school alternative.

5. *Universities Initiate Alternatives:* In Cambridge, Massachusetts, Mount Pleasant, Michigan, and Madison, Wisconsin, local universities took the lead in initiating the development of alternative schools in cooperation with the local public schools.

It was also found that while public schools usually initiate and develop their own alternatives, they have often incorporated existing independent free schools (Berkeley, California) and cooperated in establishing an alternative "outside" public education with the option of incorporating it into the public system if the school is successfully evaluated (Cambridge, Massachusetts).*

Certain school systems considering educational options proceed slowly, making sure that all participants understand what is involved. This includes avoiding a "better-than-thou" approach to alternatives, and providing the consumer with a "guarantee" that whatever option is selected will be legitimate.

For example, the historic Hyde Park School District, in New York, after initiating a cooperative relationship with the Faculty of Education of the State University College at New Paltz, began to consider alternative education. Committees were formed at both the senior and junior high schools.

Careful planning characterized the approach to alternatives. Great pains were taken not to label any of the proposed alternatives in such a way as to give one an advantage over the others —or to cast a stigma unintentionally. Names like "New Educa-

* *Changing Schools,* An Occasional Newsletter on Alternative Schools, No. 004, pp. 11, 12.

tion Ways" and "Open" were criticized and discarded because they implied that one alternative was "new" or "open" in comparison with the other alternative which could then have been perceived as "old" and "closed" in comparison. Obviously, the teachers and students considering each alternative needed to feel that they were in an equally legitimate educational environment.

Long hours of discussion involved teachers, parents, students, professors, administrators and school-board members. A common statement on alternatives at one school, Haviland Junior High, was assembled. Essential features—those common to all alternatives—were identified as 1) academic legitimacy, 2) heterogeneous student grouping, 3) non-terminal education, 4) learning experiences directed toward self-actualization and personal fulfillment. Also, certain common "guarantees" were made to students, teachers, and parents:

Students attending any one of the alternatives would be assured that they will be able to receive a similar form of education in subsequent programs in high school, that they can achieve a high school diploma, enter college or an appealing career, no matter which of the three alternatives they select.

Teachers should feel that the fact that alternatives exist does not demean in any way any single method of teaching but that it is recognized that several equally acceptable methods can co-exist within a single school district.

Parents and students should realize, and be convinced, if necessary, that students will have an equal opportunity for further education and, for that matter, all of life's benefits, regardless of which alternative they choose.*

The Hyde Park School District is engaged in careful planning at the writing of this book.

* Materials on Haviland Junior High School, from an unpublished memorandum developed in September 1972 by the Principal of the Haviland Junior High School.

The School District of Philadelphia gives us an idea of how alternative schools are approached and coordinated:

The Alternative Programs Project came about as the School District of Philadelphia, by the decision of the Superintendent and the Board of Education, became involved in a major reordering of priorities. Highest priority has been given to educational projects which are designed for the specific and explicit purpose of meeting special needs of students who have made inadequate adjustments to the on-going school program. These projects are referred to as "alternatives" because they afford the public school youngsters different types of educational experiences from those that have traditionally been offered and those that are currently provided by the regular School District program.

Among the broad goals for the alternative programs' thrust are these:
—to maintain youngsters who might otherwise relinquish an opportunity for formal education,
—to develop optional ways for students and teachers to relate,
—to increase opportunity for students to manage their own learning experience,
—to address personal problems of youngsters which may directly, or indirectly, interfere with their ability and desire to learn,
—to enable pupils to explore new ways of gaining knowledge,
—to allow teachers to capitalize on their particular professional strengths in a different kind of interaction with students,
—to shape the learning environment so that it intentionally functions as a setting suitable for many educational purposes.

New Proposals

A. The Alternative Programs Project is working with forty-six proposals for new learning programs. They have been submitted by the District's Senior and Junior High Schools and have been reviewed by a Central Review Committee, consisting of Associate Superintendents, Principals, and Program Directors.
B. Generally speaking, the proposals have typically modeled themselves after open classrooms, schools without walls, mini-schools, drop-out centers, discipline crisis centers, schools within schools, schools for students with special problems, (gifted learners, aca-

demic failures, disruptive pupils, pregnant students). All proposals contain some of the following features:

1. Provides the students and their parents, with a "choice," i.e., the freedom to choose between educational options.
2. Has a program or curriculum that is significantly different from the conventional or regular program.
3. Is a total program, not just a short class or a part of the school day.
4. Has a location, whether in a separate building, wing of a school, a community facility, or a few designated classrooms so it can be identified geographically from the regular school program.
5. Clearly defines the student population to be served.
6. Has a strong program design evidencing a creative perception of learning and instruction.
7. Demonstrates that the various school resources will be integrated into the project.
8. Builds-in the wherewithal to respond to needs of target population.
9. Establishes a connection between problem definition, the type of student selected and the program design.
10. Provides a functional relationship between the off-site unit and the home school.
11. Includes a re-entry mechanism for students to the regular school program.
12. Has a guidance and counseling focus.
13. Has an evaluation design which provides for formal monitoring and evaluation of the programs by the Research Division, as well as continuing internal evaluation and feedback.
14. Uses community, parents, mental health and welfare.

C. An important portion of the Alternative Programs Project was the formation of the Alternative Programs Office (A. P. O.). The purposes of A. P. O. are:

1. To monitor and supervise existing and newly developed Alternative Programs.
2. To develop evaluation procedures for the alternative programs.
3. To serve as consultant, facilitator, and advocate for alternative program leadership.
4. To collect information and prepare alternative program reports for the Superintendent and Board.

5. To coordinate all aspects of alternative programs as related to District Superintendents and Associate Superintendents.
6. To encourage the development of alternative programs which will be based on the "needs assessments" of the school districts; and will include programs designed to help in the areas of alienation of youth, basic skills, human relationships, motivation, career development, and attendance.
7. To introduce and expand the most effective alternatives on a system-wide basis.
8. To introduce alternative program ideas to the broader system.
9. To encourage the continuation of idea generation in the area of alternative programs.
10. To serve as a "clearing house" for experimentation, innovation, and alternative program ideas.*

The documentation of alternatives that are being implemented often are helpful to others contemplating this type of reform. Some new programs have already been documented in published books, such as the Parkway Program in Philadelphia (The School Without Walls).†

Another case study has been developed by David L. Johnston, who is with the Alternative High School in Racine, Wisconsin:

*Strategies in Developing and Implementing
an Alternative School: Racine, Wisconsin*

BACKGROUND:

Writing this description of the planning and development of the Alternative High School in Racine, Wisconsin is intended to be just that: a description, not a prescription. I do think that there is value in a description of a specific plan of how an alternative came to the stage of implementation in a public school system. The value lies in the generalizability of certain change strategies to new situations with the understanding that each new situation calls for adaptation and selec-

* From *Secondary School Alternative Programs: Existing and Newly Funded*, School District of Philadelphia, January 1973, pp. 1–3.
† See John Bremer and Michael von Moschzisker, *The School Without Walls*.

tion of those strategies. It is with this in mind that the case study of the development of the Racine Alternative High School is offered.

In the beginning of the 1971–72 school year my colleague Jack Parker and I were simultaneously completing work on our Ph.D.'s at the University of Wisconsin–Milwaukee, seven years of high school teaching and wondering in what way we could bring our teaching experience, schooled knowledge and personal interests to bear on the community of Racine, Wisconsin. It was clear that the time had come to quit talking about the changes required in education and to start acting. Our interests in continuing to teach, alternative education, the Racine community and university work that ends up in people's lives and not just on a library shelf led us to decide on planning and implementing an alternative high school that would have its sources in open education, interdisciplinary studies, community learning, pluralism and self-identification processes.

PROCEDURES:

The process of gaining final school board acceptance of the Alternative High School was achieved in May of 1972. It is to the methodology of gaining that approval that I now turn. As in many school systems across the country we faced a school board that was trying to please every frustrated section of the community and alienating them all. The community had voted down bond referendums four times in as many years. There was growing hostility between the professional teaching organization and the school board. And finally, what had once been a soundly innovative school system was now one that was trying to live off its past glories. With this array of hostile circumstances facing us we decided to plan for an alternative high school. The decision was based, in part, on the notion that times of crisis create fertile grounds for change that is planned with political and economic feasibility in mind. It is during these times that people are willing to reach out for resolutions to problems. The track is to provide a positive handle instead of a negative one for them to reach out for. With this crisis strategy as a starting point we proceeded to articulate for ourselves a set of working principles within which we would operate as we planned the school. To this end we identified the following:

1. The best-laid plans are useless without a sincere, almost selfless commitment to carrying them out.
2. Trust and credibility are gained through what you do.
3. Double talk and chicanery do confuse issues and eventually confuse those who deal in them.

4. It is not necessary to tear down what exists to create something new, as the tearing down consumes too much energy.

5. Being knowledgeable, assertive and confident does not mean one has to be overbearing and strident.

6. Educators don't have a corner on the market of what there is to know about educational needs.

7. Don't create a "they" and spend your time thinking about why "they" will never allow you to do what it is you want to do.

8. Clear and precise information allows people to make reasonable decisions. In other words, if people are kept in the dark they will act like people in the dark!

9. Planning meetings become pooled ignorance when direction for them is lacking.

10. Write it and then say it. This serves to get academic cobwebs out and protects you against misinterpretations at a later date.

11. A sense of the absurd helps one get through the day.

12. If you are taking people someplace make sure you know where you are going. One of the things we did was write a 50-page philosophical statement that served as a framework for planning.

13. Don't build a monument to your ego.

14. Expect little and hope for a great deal.

With these principles agreed upon we took the next step, which was to prepare ourselves for organizing to get school board acceptance of the Alternative High School plan and to organize people to assist in planning. For both situations we identified the political nature of change by examining the processes that brought about change in other sectors of the Racine community and adapted them to our needs. While it was worthwhile to examine the theoretical nature of political process in other communities we found it particularly valuable to analyze it in Racine, for there are political nuances that are peculiar to every community and it is these that often determine political outcomes.

Secondly, we familiarized ourselves with the history of alternatives similar to ours, those that developed in similar size school systems and research reports on open models of education. It was necessary to do this so that when the "for sure" questions of, "Do students learn anything?" "Has it been tried before?" or "Is this another radical experiment?" came up, we would be able to respond with more than personal conviction and also educate the questioners.

Thirdly, we identified where the power was and wasn't in the school bureaucracy so that we could act efficiently and appropriately. This was accomplished by identifying through personal history, pet projects, votes and public statements who made decisions and what the nature of those decisions were. After having identified the sources of power within the institution we acted on our understanding that institutions support one another by getting written letters of support for the Alternative High School plan from universities, colleges, local community organizations, and the Wisconsin State Department of Public Instruction. Through meeting personally with officials from these various institutions we got letters of support that said what we felt was necessary for the institution to say. In other words, letters of support should do more than say it's a good idea! These letters served us well throughout the rest of the year.

Fourthly, whenever possible, personal contacts were made to explain the idea of the Alternative High School to those people in the community who effected influence over various local sectors in Racine. These people were identified through personal knowledge, other persons' recommendations and close reading of the local newspaper to pick up names of people we might otherwise have overlooked. The effect of these contacts was indirect because it was through these people that supportive word for the school was spread in social and civic circles that were directly inaccessible to us.

Finally we discovered early that by referring to the Alternative High School plan in the affirmative, before its actual approved acceptance, it rather quickly became fixed in the minds of people that it was institutionally accepted. This led to interesting discussions when people argued against the plan that was not accepted as if it were. The net effect was that it gave a strong identification to the school in a sort of institutional *a priori* fashion.

STRATEGIES:

It is obvious that while what has been identified so far as strategies employed to bring the alternative high school plan toward acceptance by the school board were underway, other events were happening simultaneously, and it is to those that I now turn.

The argument for the alternative would need to be based on levels of acceptability to the community without jeopardizing the nature of the alternative. Analysis of previous educational programs related to instruction and organization that the school board rejected clearly showed that most often additional cost and lack of philosophical clarity were what defeated them. Therefore the proposal for the Alternative High School rested on two footings that defused contentious criticism of it. First, it would operate within the budget of the school system and secondly, it would be a choice made voluntarily by students who desired to attend. It was pointed out that if people pay taxes to support education, then it was in the best American tradition to give clients choices in the ways their children go to school. Pluralism is a sound argument for alternatives, especially if it doesn't cost more and occurs through a process of consent and involvement of those the alternative affects.

In preparing to go to the school board we continued to carry on the activities previously mentioned, but as the school board meeting drew near we began to make specific plans for dealing directly with the board. We decided to approach the board in two phases. At the first meeting with the board we would describe the plan and request approval for continued planning but not request approval to implement. The request for approval to implement would be made at the second meeting, which would be when we thought the time was right.

The rationale behind first asking for approval to continue planning, but not to implement was that if the board said yes, in effect they would be giving tacit approval to the idea and therefore we could begin to use the media and organize teachers, students, and parents under school board sanction of continued planning. If the board said no, we could continue to work informally on the project. In either case, the plan would not be dead!

As insurance for a yes vote at the first meeting with the board we arranged an informal meeting with the board of education and various community leaders at the Johnson Foundation of Racine, Wisconsin. We invited them to meet with us, Dr. James MacDonald and Professor Charity James to hear of alternative education developments in general and the Racine Alternative High School plan specifically. Dr. Mac-Donald and Professor James were helpful in assisting us in establishing credibility of the expert variety for the Alternative High School. This informal meeting with board members and others proved extremely valuable, since when we met with the board in formal session, they had a familiarity with the plan and, more importantly, had a sense of who we were. Surprising a board of education is most dangerous for those who surprise it. Suffice it to say the board approved continued planning.

With board approval behind us we could use the media without undermining board authority. The word "use" connotes, probably, self-serving, but we found the media extremely helpful in making the community at large aware of the Alternative High School plan and in getting people to express interest in helping develop the school. Through use of radio, talk shows, newspaper editorials and articles, we got to speak with and enlist support from groups such as the Chamber of Commerce. (Too often business groups are overlooked, when, in fact, the students who are going to the school may well have parents who are members and it is also these people who can open up community resource doors.) These engagements, although time-consuming, further the identification process of a project and result in more media exposure.

Once the plan had been approved we decided we would move forward in identifying parents and students who would be interested in the Alternative High School. The previous work with community groups, school officials and the process of gaining media exposure had given parents and students a framework for involvement and created interest in what the alternative idea was and how it could relate to them. Therefore, identification of those parents and students who were interested was attempted by a mass mailing with follow-up radio spots inviting them to a meeting that would explain the Alternative High School philosophy and plan. Two hundred parents showed up, but few students. We anticipated areas of concern that parents would have concerning the school and prepared to deal with each. Again, this was where our previous homework paid off in helping parents to understand what was proposed and to alleviate the fears they had for their children's futures. I think it is important to remember that school systems have gained approval for what goes on in schools by creating fear in parents, keeping them ignorant, overpowering them with experts and generally treating them in a paternalistic manner. The areas of parents' concern we dealt with were not programmatic but pragmatic ones framed in the following questions:

1. Will my child get into college if he goes to this school?
2. Will my child be able to get a job if he goes to this school?
3. Will students learn as much in this school?
4. Is this school for dumb and/or bad students?

Answering the first two questions was made easy through the letters of support we had gained from both colleges and the Chamber of

Commerce which indicated that the alternative program would not endanger the future plans of students and in fact might help them more than a traditional program. The last two questions required responses that came from philosophical and pedagogical insights. Educational philosophy is important for parents and students provided it has reference to the lives of the people it is explained to.

As I said earlier not many students showed up for the mass meeting and it was after a second meeting with similar results that we identified the problem that was feared at first to be lack of student interest: namely, that students do not respond to the written words emanating from establishment sources. Therefore to get the word to students about the possibility of putting an Alternative High School in their future, we set up information centers during lunch periods at the high schools, developed a cadre of student recruiters and in a general way inserted ourselves into the student grapevine. In this manner we explained the alternative idea and pre-enrolled students.

We required that parents sign an approval clause on the pre-enrollment form. This was done to clear legal problems that might occur later, because we felt if the students' parents didn't approve of their being in the school that the burden would be too great to bear on the part of the student and the Alternative High School, and that a minimum of teacher-parent, student-parent, Alternative High School-parent hassles would be needed during the first year of operations. We also felt that students by explaining the school to their parents to gain approval would better understand why they wanted to be in it. Around a thousand students took pre-enrollment forms and two hundred secured parental approval. Our goal had been 175 students representing a cross section of the Racine community. We got both the numbers and the cross section.

Early in the planning for the Alternative High School we had met with teachers to explain our idea and to ask that those who were interested in being involved join us. Periodic meetings were called thereafter to discuss and implement their ideas for planning and wherever possible to do things like contacting community resource people.

In the early phases of planning with teachers we found that it is difficult for people to deal with what was a highly ambiguous situation in planning for a school with no assurances for its implementation. This situation prevailed among those teachers and students working with us from the beginning. To offset the ambiguity of the situation and the concomitant malaise we organized through the auspices of the University of Wisconsin-Milwaukee a credit/non-credit course in alternative education which students, teachers, parents, and school board members could attend. The course brought together in microcosm for the first time the various segments of the community that would be involved directly in the Alternative understandings developed in the course helped people to decide whether the alternative form of education proposed was of interest to them and resulted in a process of self-selection as to whether to continue or discontinue involvement in planning the school. The course also became a place to experiment with instructional and organizational ideas that might be tried in the school. Individuals in the course were also extremely helpful in continuing to spread the word about the Alternative High School, thus giving it a further dimension of reality before it was in fact. Throughout our planning we identified it as absolutely necessary to keep the idea of the school uppermost in the minds of people in the community.

As another facet of our planning we had decided that once the board gave us approval to continue planning we would have ready beforehand grant proposals of two types. One would be for a small amount of money to cover planning expenses and the other a second larger proposal to gain monies for doing a detailed evaluation of the Alternative High School. We secured the small grant a week after the board approved further planning, probably because work had been done on securing it long in advance of the board meeting. The grant gave added credibility to our effort as it showed the school board that people were willing to put money into it. The gaining of the small grant from the highly respected Johnson Foundation would also serve to help us secure a large grant, as foundations and the Federal Government look with favor on programs that other institutions have already given money to. It should be pointed out that the Alternative High School was planned so that if no outside monies came in it could be still implemented. This was done by keeping its basic operating costs within the budget of Racine's Unified School District #1. Research had clearly shown that by having a school district bear the cost of new programs the likelihood was much greater for survival than if the program was dependent on outside sources of money for its basic operations. In other words, the school district would from the outset have more than a verbal investment in the school.*

* From *Changing Schools*, An Occasional Newsletter on **Alternative** Schools, pp. 11–17.

EARLY EVALUATIONS

Naturally, nearly all the parties interested in alternatives raise the question of evaluation: Do alternatives work? For example, parents ask, Can students of alternative schools qualify for college? Answers to such questions are basic to the process of legitimization.

While it is obviously too early to give definitive answers concerning the success of alternatives, the early returns are encouraging.

John Bremer, Parkway's first director, reported that of the nine students who made up the first graduating class of that alternative school, all went to college with little difficulty. At conferences, other directors of alternative schools report similar successes with college entry. In fact, some report colleges eager to receive graduates of alternative schools.*

Mike Hickey of the Seattle Public School Alternative Education project reports:

The ultimate impact of the alternative schools program in Seattle is uncertain at this point but some indications are clear: 3,000 more students are in school this year who were not in school last year.†

At this stage, while we wait for the results of the more formal, systematic attempts at evaluating alternative schools, we rely on testimony. It is difficult not to be influenced by a mother who in attendance at the first graduation exercises of Parkway exclaimed, almost in tears as she witnessed her daughter accepting a diploma, "This program saved her!"

* Reported by Vernon Smith, Associate Editor of *Changing Schools*, at a meeting at Indiana University, March 9, 1973.

† From *Changing Schools*, An Occasional Newsletter on Alternative Schools, No. 003, p. 5.

During this early period in the development of alternative schools and before the results of more systematic evaluations are reported, we rely a great deal on the testimony of the students who attend alternative schools:

As long as I have attended Metro, there has never been a fight. I do not know one person who doesn't like it here. I would never attend a public school after coming to Metro. All of the students here feel this way.

Our school may look like a little green army building, but you sure can't judge a book by its cover in this case. I mean we don't have a football team and if you're looking for a pep club, you're going to have to look pretty hard because we don't have one. But we do have one heck of a place to grow.

After I started Project "12," my outlook on getting an education went from negative to positive. This was a whole new experience in my life. School was now interesting, fulfilling, and very inspiring. At Project "12" the student is not a prisoner. He is his own person with his own ideas, which he is able to express and share.

Yes, we have books, but we blend them in with our rap sessions, or vice versa. Field trips are really fun. And, oh my, how we learn. Museums, parks, historical sightings are all interesting. Incidentally, we often take along picnic lunches on these trips which make the expedition fun as well as educational.

At Project "12" the students receive understanding because the teachers really show they care. Students who come to this school obviously have their reasons. The other schools just didn't cut it. Many of these kids have problems outside of school. There have been many times when I myself had a problem. I couldn't concentrate on my work. What would I do? I would talk about my problem with one of the teachers. They're always ready to listen and help if they can. It is so important to a student to know that someone cares.

The alternative school gives the rejected, put-down student a chance to rise up and become the young man or young woman he or she really is. Thousands of children, like me, need the alternative schools. With this type of education, many kids can receive the self-satisfaction and recognition they so desperately need and deserve. . . .*

* From *Changing Schools,* An Occasional Newsletter on Alternative Schools, No. 005, pp. 8–10.

In April 1972, an evaluation of Philadelphia's Parkway Program was conducted by Organization for Social and Technical Innovation (OSTI). The evaluation consisted primarily of field visits conducted over a six-month period. These field visits included interviews with participants and observations of the Parkway units.

OSTI concluded, in part:

The Parkway Program has accomplished something unique when viewed against the backdrop of our nation's urban education. Despite problems and weaknesses, Parkway has created an atmosphere in which students perceive rules and regulations not as hostile attacks upon their humanity, but as essential ingredients in creative group living. The adults who normally bear the responsibility for making and enforcing those rules are, at Parkway, frequently regarded as allies. Student acceptance of the necessity of rules and their affirmation of adults as people who can be trusted to care are notable achievements. In that open atmosphere students can accept the responsibility not only for themselves but for what happens to their units. In that environment of trust, people can really learn; students are unafraid to acknowledge ignorance; teachers receive more valid information from their students.*

Another important consideration for giving legitimacy to alternative schools is educational theory. Does the alternative have a theoretical justification? Is it based on a reputable pedagogical position?

EDUCATIONAL ALTERNATIVES AND THEORY

We have already given considerable attention to the so-called "open education" movement in this country as an indication of

* *Philadelphia's Parkway Program: An Evaluation Organization for Social and Technical Innovations,* 83 Rogers Street, Cambridge, Massachusetts, April 3, 1972, p. 73.

an important educational alternative within the boundaries of elementary and secondary public education. Open education has a theoretical base. That is, there is a conceptual framework which guides actual practice with children. To be sure, there are variations in the practice of "open education" based on a teacher's style and awareness of the "theory." The reader need only read John Dewey to grasp the "theory" of open education, including "schools without walls."

Educational alternatives are usually tied to the ideas of major thinkers and researchers in education. Naturally, these educational ideas differ. This makes the concept of alternatives in education all the more important. For instance, A. S. Neill in England developed the idea of a school based on "freedom." To Neill, individual freedom was at the heart of motivation and learning. On the basis of this idea, Neill developed a school he named Summerhill. This theory of "freedom" is described in his book *Summerhill.**

Neill and Summerhill have had an important impact on many private schools in this country. The so-called "free school" movement in this country (not the same as the civil rights "free schools," which also developed during the 1960's †) was based on Neill's idea that the learner be taken completely on his own terms. For example, at Skunk Hollow Free High school, a private school in Rockland County, New York, one of the stated objectives is "to teach anything students want to learn; to give students ownership and control of their education; to provide schooling without emotional stress to students." ‡

Public schools have usually kept "free school" notions at arm's length. To many public schoolmen, settings as free as the

---

* A. S. Neill, *Summerhill:* A Radical Approach to Child Rearing. New York, Hart Publishing Co., 1960.

† See Jonathan Kozol, *Free Schools.* Boston and New York, Houghton Mifflin, 1972.

‡ From *Action Report*, High School Principals' Service, August 1971.

Summerhill type are "chaotic" and "laissez-faire" environments in which the goals of education are really left to chance. This attitude has kept the Summerhill schools outside the range of public education. "Open education" is to the "right" of the free-school philosophy and much more "acceptable" in the public education sector.

Though Neill's theory is regarded with skepticism, there are other theories and philosophies of education which can become bases for generating legitimate alternatives in public education. Let us briefly review three of these:

MONTESSORI EDUCATIONAL THEORY

The Montessori approach has long been, for some parents and students, an alternative available outside the public schools. This approach is often found in private preschools and, more recently, even in a few public institutions. While the Montessori approach is not limited to the preschool level, most application of it so far has been at that level.

Child psychologists have recognized so-called "sensitive periods"—periods when a child shows unusual interest or ability in particular activities. These critical periods occur at different times and in different sequences, even for children of the same chronological age. It is therefore felt by some to be essentially self-defeating to attempt to teach children on the basis of group instruction.

The Montessori approach can be seen as an alternative to group instruction. It stresses the creation of a "prepared environment"—a combination of very purposefully designed materials and methods, arranged so as to have an inherent order and a logic of their own—in which each child engages in activities according to his own individual drive and readiness. An observer in a Montessori classroom will find each child absorbed in a separately chosen project, enjoying the presence of other children, but not necessarily working directly with them. Thus, in this noncompetitive atmosphere, the child begins to acquire a skill of lifelong value—the ability and desire to learn by himself, without reference to the accomplishments of others.

Respect for the child's own built-in rhythm and pattern of learning is apparent also in the conduct of the Montessori teacher. Forgoing the usual dominant role of a traditional classroom teacher, the Montessori teacher is a catalytic agent, a link between the child and the apparatus he will use to learn. The teacher does not hover about the child, pressuring him to go faster, nor does she stand ready to pounce on him if he should make a mistake. She is present to predispose the child toward his natural desire to explore and discover by providing a stimulating learning environment and by assisting the child in graduated exercises which do not overwhelm but challenge him and this encourages him to achieve success.

Although the materials and exercises appear simple and game-like, they are in fact well-conceived, programmed activities. Exercises in the practical affairs of life—pouring liquids, washing tables, and manipulating zippers, snaps, and buttons—enable the child to enjoy the sense of well-being, of coordinated movement, and to discover the self-fulfillment of work. There are sensorial exercises too, such as the silence game, which provides the child with a test of control of his own impulses, and the cylinder block series, which requires judgment as to increasing diameter and depth. These cylinder blocks are typical of many Montessori materials in that they have a built-in control of error. If the child errs, he knows immediately—the cylinder will not fit properly into the block. Montessori materials stress learning through movement; the manipulation of geometric forms, for example, mirrors the psychological process of the child's mind as he mentally reviews the shape, texture, and weight of the object. Apparatus is constructed to isolate a single concept, such as *long* and *short, square* and *circular,* from the distracting conditions which usually surround it.

The experiences a child has in the Montessori environment enable him to acquire patterns of independence, confidence, and concentration which are the foundation for a lifetime of creative learning.

JEAN PIAGET'S THEORIES

Some schools, breaking from tradition, have been developing programs centered on the developmental theory of Jean Piaget. Piaget's concept of development can be summarized in the six following generalizations:

1. There is an absolute continuity of all developmental processes.
2. Development proceeds through a continuous process of generalization and differentiation.
3. This continuity is achieved by a continuous unfolding. Each level of development finds its roots in a previous phase and continues into the following one.
4. Each phase entails a repetition of processes of the previous level in a different form of organization (*schema*). Previous behavior patterns are sensed as inferior and become part of the new superior level.
5. The differences in organizational pattern create a hierarchy of experience and actions.
6. Individuals achieve different levels within the hierarchy, although ". . . there is in the brain of each individual the possibility for all these developments, but they are not all realized." *

These six generalizations, as Piaget illustrates in his writings, can be set in a continuum by a division into three major phases:

* Henry W. Maier, *Three Theories of Child Development.* New York, Harper and Row, 1969, p. 102.

1. The sensorimotor phase (roughly ages 0–2).
2. The period of preparation for conceptual thought (roughly ages 2–11 or 12).
3. The phase of cognitive thought (roughly from age 11 to 12 on up).*

The ages given are of course no more than crude groupings, although individual rates of development do tend to coincide with Piaget's arbitrary ranges.

Piaget further categorizes these stages as follows:

Stage 1 describes those children who cannot answer the questions because they do not understand the principles involved.

Stage 2 is a transitional phase, characterized by groping—answers are sometimes correct, sometimes incorrect.

Stage 3 is for those who give a correct response and show by their explanations a firm grasp of the concepts involved.†

The implication of Piaget's developmental theory has most recently been seen in laboratory settings. For the purpose of our discussion, we cite its use in math. Many teachers have set up what they thought of as a laboratory situation as part of their mathematics program—for example, playing store. But on the basis of Piaget's research, Richard Copeland comments:

Such procedures are, however, still not a laboratory learning situation in terms of an individualized approach to learning: they are usually a total class endeavor with the whole class doing or attempting to do the same problems at the same time. For some, it has meaning; for others, it does not.‡

A true laboratory situation should allow for individual work as a basis for learning with emphasis on meaning:

* *Ibid.,* p. 103.

† Leonard Marsh, *Alongside the Child: Experiences in the English Primary School.* New York, Harper and Row, 1972, p. 15.

‡ Richard W. Copeland, *How Children Learn Mathematics: Teaching Implications of Piaget's Research.* New York, The Macmillan Company, 1970, p. 167.

In a laboratory situation, children may be given "assignment" cards that are usually problems that require using some of the materials in the math laboratory. There is much measuring, comparing, sorting, and questioning.

Assignments may be on an individual basis or in the form of some type of grouping. Allowing children to work in pairs provides for much first-hand experience and also allows opportunity for discussion of the problem. In experiments, one child may perform and the other record. After evaluating their findings, they decide on the best way of making a record of their findings; for example, a graph, model or table. While pairing or grouping is important for vocabulary development and sharing ideas, it may mean that only one person is learning and the other simply following. The teacher can observe easily enough and make grouping changes as necessary. It may be advisable to make grouping changes as new assignments are undertaken.

Children may be grouped by friendship, mixed ability, or common ability. Each has its advantages and disadvantages. The Piaget experiments can serve as a basis for determining common ability groups.*

If learning is to be on an individual basis with actual rather than vicarious experience:

. . . a different physical arrangement of the classroom is necessary. Also a more permissive classroom atmosphere must exist. Children should be allowed to move about as they seek answers to questions.†

As the statement above indicates, innovation in teaching approaches as well as in classroom organization follows when the teachers begin to adjust to the developmental theories of Piaget as a basis for planning their instructional programs.

The implications of Piaget's theories, of course, have not yet been fully developed. When they are, they should bring about more innovative approaches to instruction, thus providing new options for the educational consumer.

* *Ibid.*, pp. 268–270.
† *Ibid.*, p. 271.

BEHAVIOR MODIFICATION AND ANALYSIS

Behavior Analysis or Behavior Modification involves token reinforcement systems of learning. It is based on the theories of certain psychologists—for example, B. F. Skinner of Harvard—and is being used in several school districts including those in New York, Massachusetts, Missouri, and Illinois. Under the umbrella of Behavior Analysis, team-teaching, nongraded classrooms, programmed instruction, and individualized teaching have been used to facilitate achievement of the objectives set up.

In a series of steps, this instructional system defines the instructional objectives of the material to be taught, and determines the degree to which the child already knows the material. Using a Special Entry Behavior Inventory and diagnostic tests, the teacher decides where each child needs to begin. At higher levels of achievement, these diagnostic tests are imbedded in the materials to insure that each child is mastering each instructional objective before being moved on to the next. On the premise that the child learns best when he is motivated, those engaged in behavior analysis emphasize the use of "positive reinforcements" or rewards.

These reinforcements (rewards, praise, etc.) are given the child immediately whenever his behavior is "good," thus reinforcing or strengthening that behavior. Because many reinforcing events are hard to deliver with the necessary immediacy, Behavior Analysis classrooms use a Token Exchange System to sustain a high level of motivation:

. . . As each child in the class works at various learning tasks, he is given tokens for his progress and improvement. Later, after he has accumulated several tokens in this way, he has the opportunity to exchange them for events and activities which are important to him. These back-up activities give meaning and value to the tokens. As long as the back-ups are exciting and enjoyable, the tokens will support the child's motivation to learn and to succeed.

Tokens, in addition to being properly timed, must be delivered frequently to be most effective. When a child is faced with a new and difficult task, tokens are given often for small amounts of progress. At a later stage, as the child's skill improves, fewer tokens are needed to support progress. Consequently, the way a child earns tokens is constantly changing. At first, tokens and praise will follow a child's first attempt at holding a pencil correctly. Later, as skill increases, the tokens and praise will follow the writing of a complete sentence.*

The requirement of frequent attention and reinforcement for each individual is difficult, if not impossible, for one teacher to fulfill; therefore, there is a Parent Program to aid the classroom staff. Each classroom is staffed by four adults:

. . . The lead teacher heads the team and generally takes special responsibility for reading instruction. The full-time aide usually takes special responsibility for the small math groups; and two parent aides concentrate on handwriting and spelling lessons and individual tutoring. This kind of team arrangement insures that every child receives the personal attention and reinforcement needed for him to learn at his maximum rate.

. . . Parents who have worked in the classroom are also extending the benefits of the program into the home situation. With an understanding of classroom process and the principles of positive reinforcement, the parents are able to join professional teachers as partners in the education of the community's children.†

The daily schedule of a Behavior Analysis classroom can be described under three headings: planning, formal instruction, and activities or back-ups.

. . . Twenty-five to thirty children at different performance levels and four adults make a complex organization which must be carefully

---

* *The Behavior Analysis Classroom*, The University of Kansas Support and Development Center for Follow Through, 1970, p. 7.

† *Ibid.*, pp. 7–9.

managed if it is to be successful. To insure a smooth operation that is always ready to meet the changing needs of the children, a period is set aside each day for staff planning. Directed by the lead teacher, these sessions allow the classroom team to discuss specific strategies to be used with particular children, new or problematic sections of the curriculum, revisions in classroom routine, and back-up activities.

The specific lesson plan for any given day is always determined by the progress of the children. In general, however, the three core subjects are all taught during each instructional period. By providing at least three periods during the day, each child receives instruction in every subject.

Every instructional period is planned in conjunction with the back-up activity which will follow. At the beginning of a year there is frequent alternation between instruction (learning periods) and special back-ups (exchange periods). Ten to fifteen minutes of instruction, followed by twenty to twenty-five minutes of exchange activity, followed by another fifteen minutes of instruction, etc., is a common pattern. As the children become more skillful, the amount of study time increases, and the end of the year may find a schedule which provides for 45–50 minutes of study for each ten to fifteen minutes of special activity. At the second or third grade level it is not unusual for twenty minutes of contingent special activity to support an entire morning's work.*

Behavior Analysis classrooms are seen by many as lively and interesting places where there is seldom any punishment. As an alternative, they can enable children to develop good learning behavior in order to get a better education.

As we have seen, the national alternatives movement, though it is only a few years old, has already developed broadly, ranging in continuum from single public schools considering classroom options, such as "open education," to specific school districts embarking on systemwide alternatives. During the decades ahead, this movement is likely to become more and more effective with time and experience. However, alternatives cannot move ahead in a constructive manner without serious thought

* *Ibid.*, pp. 10–12.

being given to the processes by which they are made legitimate within the public schools.

But as alternative schools spring up, the question of money soon surfaces. What effect do they have on the financing of public schools? Do they cost more money? Will they pose strains on an already overburdened public school system? Since money questions nowadays are on the minds of all of us, perhaps a review of the fiscal situation is in order—with special emphasis, of course, on Public Schools of Choice.

VII / FINANCING OF PUBLIC
SCHOOLS OF CHOICE

REVIEWING THE SCHOOL FINANCE PICTURE

Would Public Schools of Choice cost more money? There is not an American property owner alive who is not outraged by the rising costs of education; even the most fanatic supporters of school reform are profoundly discouraged by the financial demands of educational progress. Everyone wants quality education for his children, but the costs seem prohibitive.

It is my contention that Public Schools of Choice need not and, indeed, should not cost more money. Instead, it calls primarily for a *redistribution of existing public school resources, and a more efficient use of the funds we have already been allotted.*

During the past decade the American public has poured out billions in new money to improve education. The results have not been encouraging. Why? Primarily because this money has helped us only to do "more of the same"—to improve a monolithic system of education. Our fiscal effort has resulted in a compensatory, remedial, "add-on" strategy for school improvement. This simply has not worked for significant numbers of school-users. In short, we have increased school costs without results in increased productivity. The case of helping improve the education of economically disadvantaged children highlights the problem. President Nixon reported:

The best available evidence indicates that most of the compensatory education programs have not measurably helped poor children catch up.

Recent findings on the two largest such programs are particularly disturbing. We now spend more than $1 billion a year for educational programs run under Title I of the Elementary and Secondary Education Act. Most of these have stressed the teaching of reading, but before-and-after tests suggest that only 19% of the children in such programs improve their reading significantly; 13% appear to fall behind more than expected; and more than two-thirds of the children remain unaffected—that is, they continue to fall behind. In our Headstart program, where so much hope is invested, we find that youngsters enrolled only for the summer achieve almost no gains, and the gains of those in the program for a full year are soon matched by their non-Headstart classmates from similarly poor backgrounds.*

A fiscal policy reflecting this view was redefined by President Nixon just after his second-term victory:

This country has enough on its plate in the way of huge new spending programs, social programs, throwing dollars at problems. What we need is, basically, reform of existing institutions and not the destruction of our tried values in this country. Consequently, the next Administration will be one of reform, not just adding more dollars—reform of education, reform in the field of health, reform in Federal-state relations, reform in all fields . . .

Reform using money more effectively will be the mark of this Ad-

* Nixon, Richard M., "Message from the President of the United States," 91st Congress, 2d Session, Document No. 91–267, House of Representatives, March 3, 1970, p. 5.

ministration, rather than simply coming up with huge new bundles of money to throw at the problems. I don't believe that the answer to the nation's problems is simply massive new programs in terms of dollars and in terms of people . . .

The *reforms* have to be ones which will make government run better at less cost. The *reforms* also, insofar as any new programs are concerned, must be ones that are within our budget limitations . . .

The *reforms* that we are instituting are ones which will diffuse the power throughout the country and which will make government leaner, but in a sense will make it stronger. After all, fat government is weak, weak in handling the problems . . .

We are going to change the way we are going to do this and rather than government doing more for people and making people more dependent upon it, what I am standing for is government finding ways through the government programs *to allow people to do more for themselves,* to encourage them to do more for themselves; not only encourage them, but to give them incentive to do more for themselves on their own without government assistance.*

Putting new money into an outdated educational system for remedial programs can result at best in a slightly improved but still *outdated* system. The problem calls for more responsive, more productive utilization of existing human and material resources. Any new money should be used as conversion capital to reform our public schools. Again, President Nixon makes the issue clear: "American education is in urgent need of reform." †
Alternative education, through a different utilization of existing resources, can begin to effect this reform.

Before we can make a case for the economic feasibility of Public Schools of Choice, it will be useful to review the economic structure of American education. *It would be erroneous to imply that the existing system of public school finance is a desirable one.* Although we recommend that Public Schools of

* Nixon, Richard M., President, in an exclusive interview published in the *Washington Evening Star* and *Daily News,* November 9, 1972.

† Education Message from the President of the United States to the Congress, March 3, 1970.

Choice ask for no additional monies, it is clear that reform in school finance in general is mandatory. The financial burdens on the American taxpayer have served to undermine school reform, regardless of the support given quality education. Soon monetary pressures will have conditioned the voter to reject any plan for school improvement on the simple basis of finance.

Therefore, it is the reform of public school financing that must be tackled. In pragmatic terms, it is clear that such reform requires a great deal of time. In addition, reforming school finances is two-dimensional: to find more equitable formulae for school revenue, and to find more effective and efficient ways to use existing money. In the meantime, it is imperative that new plans be implemented to improve the quality of education for millions of Americans who are being denied it in our present set-up.

Second only to defense public education in the United States is our most expensive institution. One-fourth of our population —fifty million people—are connected with public schools, and they consume one-tenth of the national income. Education is now being financed primarily on a state and local level.

FEDERAL AND STATE SUPPORT OF EDUCATION, AND LOCAL CONTROL

Public schools, unlike the agencies of the Defense Department, are not controlled by the federal government. The historical roots of local control of public education can be traced to the Constitution, which delegated power over education to the individual states. In turn, the states have relinquished much of their control to local districts.

The principle of local control of public schools is thus one of the basic tenets of American public education. But this political gift has had its price, and neighborhoods have had to carry the costs of their local schools. Finally, in the 60's, federal aid to education was both legalized and made acceptable as a subsidy to less prosperous areas in this country. In 1967, however, only 8 percent of the total cost of public education was borne by the federal government; the bulk of the cost has remained a local matter—30 percent of the cost was provided by the states that year, and 54 percent came from local districts, almost exclusively the product of property taxes. In 1900, the number of local districts was close to 130,000; in 1970, as a result of consolidation, the figure was closer to 19,000.*

The importance of education to American society is reflected in the astounding rise in expenditures for public education. In twenty years, school spending increased nearly fivefold. In 1950, school spending was not quite 2 percent of the gross national product: by 1970, it had risen to 10 percent. These figures apply only to the educational costs of public elementary and secondary schools; the figures would be even greater if the 12 percent of the population using private schools were also included.

The financing of public schools is derived from three principal sources of funding: at the local level primarily from property taxes, at the state level from various corporate, sales, and personal income taxes, and at the federal level from individual and corporate income taxes. To all intents and purposes, the property tax provides most of the money for American education. And, at the heart of local public school revenues, the property tax represents the largest single source of revenue for all state and local government. Property taxes, we have pointed out, provide 54 percent of all public school revenues; over 98 percent of the public school revenues from local tax sources are property tax revenues.†

* *NEA Research Bulletin,* Volume 48, No. 2, May 1970, National Education Association, Washington, D.C., p. 38.

† *Annual Report of the Council of Economic Advisers,* Government Printing Office, Washington, D.C., 1969, p. 144.

One of the key problems associated with the property tax is that the ratio of assessed values to full legitimate values has declined, thereby reducing significantly the capacity of a school district to tap local funds on a continuous basis. This problem becomes more acute with the rise in school costs caused by inflation, mandated salary schedules, etc.

We have reached a stage in which even the most staunch supporters of public education have been affected by this overdependence on the local property tax. Citizens simply cannot continue to have their taxes raised indefinitely on the ground that lack of the additional revenue would deprive their children of quality education. Obviously, there is a limit to what the taxpayer can afford, and we are now pressing hard on this limit. The outcome can only be injurious to both the citizen and the public school.

The so-called taxpayers' revolt is already in high momentum. One need only speak with school officials from literally any section of the nation to realize that the citizen has begun to call a halt to increased taxation of his property for public school improvement.

However, while there is indeed a general mood of discontent with overreliance on the property tax for financing public schools, there is another dimension which may actually become the legal basis for reform: the fact that the property tax within most states results in an unequal allocation of educational resources, and thus arbitrarily discriminates against the poor. That is to say, since property taxes are assessed according to wealth, "richer" communities receive more revenues than communities which are less affluent. Thus "privileged" public school districts can actually afford better delivery of educational services than tional resources was considered by some citizens to be *uncon-* poor school districts. This inequality in the allocation of *educa-* *stitutional* on the grounds that the property tax system for financing public schools actually denies some children the equal protection guaranteed under the Fourteenth Amendment, and they appealed to the courts.

In an historic decision the Supreme Court of California, on August 30, 1971, tentatively concluded:

We have determined that this funding scheme invidiously discriminates against the poor because it makes the quality of a child's education a function of the wealth of its parents and neighbors. Recognizing as we must that the right to an education in our public schools is a fundamental interest which cannot be conditioned on wealth, we can discern no compelling state purpose necessitating the present method of financing. We have concluded, therefore, that such a system cannot withstand constitutional challenge and must fall before the equal protection clause.

The decision in this case (*Serrano vs. Priest*) has launched a national dialogue on the inequities of the local property tax. The Plaintiffs in the California case were Los Angeles County public school children and their parents "who pay real property taxes in the county of their residence."

The Plaintiff's complaint alleged that the California financing scheme:

A. Makes the quality of education for school age children in California, including Plaintiff Children, a function of the wealth of the children's parents and neighbors, as measured by the tax base of the school district in which said children reside, and
B. Makes the quality of education for school age children in California, including Plaintiff Children, a function of the geographical accident of the school district in which said children reside, and
C. Fails to take account of any of the variety of educational needs of the several school districts (and of the children therein) of the State of California, and
D. Provides students living in some school districts of the State with material advantages over students in other school districts in selecting and pursuing their educational goals, and
E. Fails to provide children of substantially equal age, aptitude, moti-

vation, and ability with substantially equal educational resources, and

F. Perpetuates marked differences in the quality of educational services, equipment and other facilities which exist among the public school districts of the State as a result of the inequitable apportionment of State resources in past years.

G. The use of the "school district" as a unit for the differential allocation of educational funds bears no reasonable relation to the California legislative purpose of providing equal educational opportunity for all school children within the State.

H. The part of the State financing scheme which permits each school district to retain and expend within that district all of the property tax collected within that district bears no reasonable relation to any educational objective or need.

The Plaintiffs offer the example:

... In Los Angeles County, where Plaintiff children attend school, the Baldwin Park Unified School District spent only $577.49 to educate each of its pupils in 1968–1969; during the same year, the Pasadena Unified School District spent $840.19 on every student; and the Beverly Hills Unified School District paid out $1,231.72 per child. The source of these disparities is unmistakable: in Baldwin Park, the assessed valuation per child totaled only $3,706; in Pasadena, assessed valuation was $13,706; while in Beverly Hills, the corresponding figure was $50,885, a ratio of 1 to 4 to 13.

... Furthermore, basic aid, which constitutes about half of the state educational funds, actually widens the gap between rich and poor districts. Such aid is distributed on a uniform per pupil basis to all districts irrespective of the district's wealth, Beverly Hills, as well as Baldwin Park, receiving $125 from the state for each of its students.

Harold Howe, former United States Commissioner of Education and now Vice President of the Ford Foundation, sensing the major implications of the Serrano Case, advances two models for equalizing school finance through greater state responsibility:

One consists of the relations between state universities and colleges and state educational authorities in the United States. While these differ from state to state, most state authorities trust campus professionals to run their own affairs. State universities, for example, can hire their own teachers without an elaborate licensing or certification system, and they can plan their own curricular offerings and methods of teaching. State approval is required only when a totally new activity or department is involved. On the other hand, the state does the planning to avoid duplication, control costs, and guarantee services. This spirit could apply in a revised state system of schooling with fewer and larger school districts.

The second model is Britain's system of publicly supported schools. Local schools get most of their funds from the central Ministry of Education, yet they are fiercely independent and operate individual programs. The ministry maintains an "Inspectorate," but inspectors typically play a role that belies their title. They are not authority figures whose business is to check on the minutiae of administrative practice. They are stimulators of change and improvement, communication agents who disseminate good practice by persuasion, and experienced educators and teachers—rather than officious bureaucrats.[*]

Howe also raises the two problems of control and diversity. Will full state funding mean greater control by the state, with greater uniformity in education? The first problem, that of control, is handled by the structure of the models themselves. A more tricky issue for Howe is diversity, which he considers a positive value. Public Schools of Choice does speak directly to the problem of diversity. If the public schools can commence their journey toward diversity now, they will have a base to withstand any normal pressure toward homogenization, such as might accompany a change in the financing of public education.

In January, 1972, New Jersey State Superior Court Judge Theodore I. Botter held that the state's school-tax system, based heavily on local property taxes, violated the equal-education and equal-protection guarantees of the state constitution, as well as the equal protection provisions of the United States Constitution (the equal protection clause of the Fourteenth Amendment).

[*] Harold Howe, 2nd, "Anatomy of a Revolution," in *Saturday Review*, November 20, 1971, pp. 84–88.

Judge Botter said the system ". . . discriminated against poor people in the city and against taxpayers in general because it made them bear unequal tax burdens to pay for a common state purpose—education." *

PROPOSALS FOR REFORM

In New York State, the Governor-appointed Commission on the Quality, Cost, and Financing of Elementary and Secondary Schools, influenced by the Serrano Case, recommended basic reform in the state school financing policies. The Fleischmann Commission (named after its chairman, Manly Fleischmann, a Buffalo lawyer) reported in January of 1972. The 18-man commission released its proposal for fall school funding after two years of study, involving sixty consultants. New York State now provides about 45 percent of the five billion a year spent on the public schools, the federal government about 4 percent, and the local communities the remainder. Under Commission proposals, the state would take over the raising and distribution of all non-federal funds for its public schools, mainly by means of a uniform statewide property tax replacing local education levies. Thus it would achieve the greater parity between rich and poor districts which is its main objective. The statewide property tax would be set at about $2.04 per $100 of true value—a rate designed to yield approximately the amount now raised locally for schools.

The Fleischmann report emphasized the point that at the present time some wealthier districts in the state spend as much as $2700 per pupil, while some poor districts spend as little as $860. The commission recommended therefore that the level of spending of a majority of the state's 769 districts be raised, while

* News report in *The New York Times*, January 21, 1972.

the level of the wealthier districts remained frozen. The Fleischmann proposals would thus within three years raise the per-pupil expenditures of two-thirds of the school districts in the state, some 474 districts. The commission proposals would permit a "levelling up" of the poor districts, but not "levelling down" of the wealthier ones. This, it is felt, would set it against a "least common denominator" imposed by central controls.

The problem of school financing has now reached the highest levels of public policy—the President of the United States and the Supreme Court. In his State of the Union Message to a Joint Session of Congress in January 1972 President Nixon announced that the government was seeking new ways of financing public schools to replace the traditional, overburdened method of relying on local property taxes.

President Nixon and his staff have been studying the concept of a value added tax * as a means of raising revenues to pay for local schools. The "value added tax" under study is a form of national sales tax in which a tax is collected on the "value added" to the product at each level of production. Each seller of a product gets credit for the amount he has paid to the manufacturer or processor ahead of him by deducting that amount from the tax he is required to pay on his own sale. Such a national sales tax would theoretically permit a cut in local property tax; it would be tied to a national revenue sharing plan. While a value added tax might indeed raise new revenues (it is estimated that a 10 percent tax on the total United States output would mean a yield of close to 100 billion dollars), of which a great deal might conceivably go to education, the burden of the tax falls in the end on the consumer. That may be its biggest flaw.

One or another type of value added tax is already in operation in various Western nations: France, West Germany, the

* "A New Tax Under Study" in *U.S. News and World Report*, June 21, 1971, p. 27.

Netherlands, Luxembourg, Belgium, Brazil, Denmark, Norway and Sweden.

In January of 1973, President Nixon's Budget Message outlined his intent to move toward revenue sharing in education. The general idea behind revenue sharing is for the federal government to make block grants to the states which, in cooperation with local governments, would be free to determine how the funds would be utilized.

This was followed with the introduction of a special revenue-sharing bill called Better Schools Act in the late spring of 1973. This act consolidates some thirty categorized aid programs into five broad categories: the disadvantaged, vocational education, the handicapped, assistance to school districts with large numbers of federal employees living on federal property, and supportive educational services (textbooks, school lunches, etc.).

The 2.7 billion dollar bill was the subject of much congressional debate. Questions relating to the equity of formulas that would concentrate the bulk of the aid to school districts with disadvantaged populations would leave no aid to other districts also interested in reform.*

The other historic case, *Rodriguez v. San Antonio Independent School District,* which also challenges the constitutionality of the property tax financing system in Texas, was considered by the United States Supreme Court.

On March 21, 1973, the Supreme Court, by a five to four vote, upheld the constitutionality of the Texas school finance system. The bare majority ruling concluded that state laws for financing public schools should not be considered unconstitutional "merely because the burdens or benefits thereof fall unevenly, depending upon the relative wealth of the political subdivisions in which citizens live." †

* *The New York Times,* March 22, 1973.
† *Ibid.*

Prior to the Supreme Court decision, a number of states influenced by the *Serrano* and *Rodriguez* cases had begun to evaluate their school financing methods.

In early 1973, California enacted a $1.1 billion tax reform school-aid bill that increases the State's contribution to local school districts from 35 to 50 per cent over several years. The bill allocates funds to school districts according to an equalization formula that gives more money to districts with lower assessed property value. Ohio has changed its state aid formula in an attempt to promote greater equalization. Other states, also, are in the process of reviewing their state aid formulas.

One of the underlying reasons for not rejecting the property taxes is the fear of weakening the principle of local control in education. This fear was the major deterrent to federal aid to education during the first half of this century. Even when federal aid was introduced, the principle of local control remained a paramount criterion. Keeping public education close to the citizens—especially the family—is a basic force in the school financing picture. President Nixon emphasized this point in his 1972 State of the Union message when he stated that all school finance recommendations made by any special presidential commission "will be rooted in one fundamental principle with which there can be no compromise: local school boards must have control over local schools."

Government financing and control of education also generates concern that such centralization will lead to greater uniformity and conformity.

This is one of the main appeals of Public Schools of Choice. Not only do the decisions about education remain local, but uniformity is replaced by diversity.

In one sense, while reforms in school financing are being considered, localities are left with the problem of making the best out of whatever educational resources they have on hand. One equitable way to deal with this without compromising the value of keeping education decisions close to the individual citizen is to consider alternative education by choice.

The entire school finance picture remains confused. We are in a period of transition. However, taxpayers and politicians are increasingly concerned with productivity for each dollar invested in education. They are interested in reform. While the search for a more equitable fiscal policy continues, the localities continue to endure the bulk of the school costs. At a time of rising costs, this poses increased pressure on the homeowners who gradually press for relief. This process has led to a "get tough" mood concerning the schools—a challenging of established practices, a review of fiscal effectiveness. In New York State, for example, it has led to a proposal by the Governor to establish an Inspector General for education who would be responsible for establishing better fiscal efficiency.

In the meantime, public schools need to reform themselves with the resources that they have on hand. The road toward continuous add-on reform is being blocked by new public policies. New approaches to school reform are needed. Alternative education is one such approach.

Whatever method is chosen, it is clear that achieving a better basis for financing elementary and secondary schools is crucial. Otherwise, we cannot hope to support the continued development of quality education demanded by the needs of an advancing technological society. Yet, while it appears hopeful that national priorities may swing in favor of education, we are left with the immediate problem that our educational problem will not wait for new policies.

UTILIZING EXISTING RESOURCES DIFFERENTLY

Since the plan for Public Schools of Choice calls only for a different utilization of existing resources, its problem is mainly seeing to it that existing personnel—both teachers and administrators—use their talents in new ways. If there are four first-grade teachers in School A now serving X number of children, why could not one class be an "open" classroom, and the other three remain standard? Obviously, the four teachers are already working, receiving salaries, etc. The parents send their children to the school. The children are individually assigned to the four teachers in some fashion, anyway.

It is conceivable that of the four teachers, at least one might possess a style of teaching which is more congruent with generating an open classroom than are the teaching styles of the others. At present, this "open-styled" teacher simply imposes her style on her children, whether they learn in such an environment, or not, whether they prefer such a structure, or not. Parents, too, accept the policy that as long as their children are assigned to a bonafide teacher, all is well. It is from the parent who is discontented for one reason or another—perhaps because the child is not reading as fast as the other children—that complaints arise.

Yet, with a very simple change in policy, any grade in any school can provide a teacher with the opportunity to develop an alternative based on her own personal style of teaching. A shift in school policy offering a match between teacher style and learner preference—a shift from chance to choice in assignment of classes—makes all the difference in our plan—and keeps the cost the same.

At the secondary level, it is possible to have both a school with walls and an alternative—a school *without* walls—as is the case in Philadelphia with its Parkway Program. The Parkway Program,* as we have seen, was constructed as another way of providing high school students with learning opportunities.

* See: John Bremer and Michael von Moschzisker, *The School Without Walls*. Holt, Rinehart and Winston, 1971. See also Chapter V.

Many, but not all, high school students in the Philadelphia Public Schools were not responding to the standard high school approach. The Parkway Program established a different set of assumptions in which the city itself was viewed as the "classroom."

This alternative was not imposed on any existing high school, thereby jeopardizing the rights of the teachers, parents and students who did not prefer the new approach. Instead, the Parkway Program was offered to students, parents and teachers as a choice.

In this process, a group of teachers already on the payroll of the School District of Philadelphia were selected for the Program. Similarly, a group of 130 or so students who were attending high schools in the district were selected. They came together without making use of any existing high school building.

By using the resources of the community—the Franklin Institute, the Art Museum, and so on—this School Without Walls may be said to have saved the School District and its taxpayers an estimated twenty million dollars on construction costs alone! That is to say, if the traditional pattern had been followed, the School District might simply have requested more money for the construction of a new high school. Under the Parkway Program, no money was requested. The alternative high school used existing resources—teachers, clerks, administrators and the facilities of the city itself. Bremer and von Moschzisker report on what the Parkway Program meant fiscally:

But high schools have other costs the Parkway Program does not have at all. First, there is the cost of the high school building itself. This cost, according to the most recent estimate for a three-year high school for 2000 students in Philadelphia, is not quite $20 million. Since the money has to be borrowed, the interest will amount to almost as much again. The school will therefore cost the taxpayer $40 million, and if it is earthquake-proof, it may last for forty years. The cost per year of just the building, not including instruction, heating, lighting, and so on, is $1 million. With 2000 students, the cost per year for the building alone is $500 per student. Parkway uses virtually no money for this purpose; it pays rent on one unit only for less than $60 per student per year.

It should be remembered that building costs (that is, capital expenditures) are often calculated on a per student basis, using the total number of students in the system. It may be unfair to pretend that a student in one of the very old schools shares in the benefits accruing to a student in a brand new school. However, on this basis, the per pupil cost for buildings in Philadelphia is more than $100—and the amount goes up each year. Either way it is figured, Parkway is cheaper.*

Similarly, it is possible to organize three or more high schools within an existing high school building. Since the staff and student composition remains the same, the basic change is only in conceptualizing the use of the building in a new way. As we have reported, there is a movement to create "schools within schools." One building can hold three schools, for example, each school mounted on a different educational conception from the others.

Further, as new commercial buildings are designed, space for instructional or educational purposes can be included in them. The commercial enterprise performs a "public interest first" (with obvious PR value) and opportunities for developing educational options at no extra cost are enhanced.

Consider this review of the costs involved in the mini-schools of New York:

The mini-school approach is made up of five components. Four cost nothing, or next to it, in money:

Smaller student body offers a better learning environment—less alienation, more communication between teachers and students. No extra cost, since this requires only an organizational and geographic shift of teachers and students, not an expansion.

Business participation—private-sector resources, people and experi-

* *Op. cit.*, pp. 108–9.

ence are brought into the school as educational tools. No extra cost to the taxpayer, only moderate cost to the cooperating firms.

Municipal delivery—employment of the school as a channel for existing government services (health, legal, social service, employment). No extra cost, simply a rechanneling of existing services through the schools.

Staff development—Professional Service Center, curriculum developments, teacher training. No extra cost to the taxpayer except (to a very small extent) as an American citizen, since this relatively small expenditure—one half million dollars in three years—has been assumed by a combination of Federal and private funds.

A fifth mini-school component, *streetworkers*, does cost. A little. (To be exact, about $54 per student at Haaren.) For this sum, streetworkers handle problems that range from drug usage, emotional and health problems to the housing, legal and employment needs of students and their families.*

Consider also the report on the St. Paul Open School:

Because the St. Paul Open School makes use of many volunteers and relies on students' own self-direction in many instances, the per-pupil cost is actually less than the average for the city. The school was launched with the aid of $125,200 in private grants and $100,000 in federal funds from Title III of the Elementary and Secondary Education Act, and received a Bush Foundation grant in the summer of 1972 to pay for teacher preparation.†

Further, at the Second National Conference on Educational Alternatives held in Racine, Wisconsin, it was reported:

Given the growing crisis in educational finance, conference participants were concerned with exploring possible strategies for financing public school alternatives. Once again, no single approach was found. In all of the schools, alternatives were financed by rearranging existing re-

* *Mini-School News*, Volume 2, No. 6.
† *Alternative Schools*, a publication of the National School Public Relations Association, 1972, p. 36.

sources so that the established per-pupil cost in a district became the basic cost factor. And while a number of alternatives were identified that had been funded externally by the Ford Foundation and the U.S. Office of Education (Berkeley, California; Minneapolis, Minnesota; Philadelphia, Pennsylvania), there was a growing conviction that external funding is not always needed and sometimes works to the disadvantage of the local alternative. Seattle, Washington, described how twenty-three alternatives were established by utilizing existing funds, and Grand Rapids, Michigan, explained how alternatives started on soft money, but within three years had converted the entire cost of the schools within the per-pupil cost of the school district. Cooperative funding of alternatives by several contiguous school systems suggests another model for education reform. In Elkins Park, Pennsylvania, six school systems have cooperatively financed two public school alternatives. Similar situations can be found in the Denver area and the Grand Rapids area.*

At the present time, we have an elaborate supervision network. Each school district has a central staff of supervisors, coordinators and curriculum developers, pupil-personnel specialists, and so on. Their time is spent trying to make the standard educational process work for everyone. The result is that much of their time and talent is consumed in remedial effort. For example, we have suggested that students who do not adjust to the standard school process become absentees or disrupters; as a result, extra time is spent dealing with their "symptoms." Enormous amounts of money are spent in mounting compensatory efforts. Every school district has some type of tracking system concentrating on those who diverge from the standardized norms. But the same supervisors, the same special staff, could be spending their time in helping parents, teachers, students, develop alternative forms of education.

Again, since these roles already exist, since the staff is already

* *Changing Schools*, An Occasional Newsletter on Alternative Schools, No. 004, p. 12.

receiving wages, it is not a matter of more cost, *but of a different utilization of staff.*

Developing legitimate educational alternatives also frees the "system" to explore other sources of improved learning. For example, many "options" emphasize the "learning by teaching" approach in which "children teach children." Not only does this type of activity not cost money, but many children, as tutors, learn more when performing the teaching role than when acting as students in a formal classroom.*

Certain options may involve students from nearby colleges and universities. Here, again, we have literally thousands of "teachers" or "tutors" who can be utilized on a regular basis to "individualize instruction" or to "enrich the curriculum" in our public schools. Many college students would welcome such programs. It would help colleges with their own programs, connecting campuses with communities and practical concerns.

SEEKING OUTSIDE FUNDING SOURCES: PRIVATE FOUNDATIONS AND GOVERNMENT

We must also point out that "outside" money is now available to most school districts, and these funds too could be used in new ways. For example, Title I of the Elementary and Secondary Education Act provides money to local education agencies to help educate so-called "disadvantaged" children. At present, this money is being used primarily for compensatory education. Money is used to hire extra teachers, specialists, counselors, and so on. Reasonable as compensatory education appears to be, the results to date are far from encouraging.

Could not this new federal money † be used, in part, to assist

---

* See Alan Gartner, M. Kohler, and F. Riessman, *Children Teach Children: Learning by Teaching.* New York: Harper and Row, 1971.
† See p. 210 above.

parents, students and teachers or administrators to *convert* existing schools into Public Schools of Choice?

The Berkeley Unified School District and its experiment with alternative schools attracted considerable outside support. True, outside fiscal support on this scale is usually reserved for "pioneer" efforts, for "start up" costs are necessary to offer a reasonable chance for developing prototype programs; those in turn can be disseminated to other school districts in the country. Thus, we all learn now because of money invested in Berkeley in 1970–71.

There are other federal and state-aid funds which could be similarly utilized. Title III of the Elementary and Secondary Education Act has made money available to schools for innovation. This Title does not limit the use of its funds to work with poor children; therefore, most school districts—perhaps in a regional effort—can use this money for planning and innovation.* The same can be said for much of the money available under the Educational Personnel Development Act (EPDA), the Experimental Schools Program, etc.

OEO has funded a "voucher" experiment in California which comes close to Public Schools of Choice. Faced with resistance to an "external" voucher, and in the absence of enabling state legislation, OEO decided to consider demonstration of a transitional type of voucher. This transitional voucher would involve only public schools (or private schools operating under contract to the public schools) and could serve as a pilot for an expanded voucher demonstration effort later on.

After feasibility grants had been made in five school districts, OEO decided to implement a transitional plan in the Alum Rock Public Schools (in San Jose, California) for the 1972–73 school year. Surveys conducted in Alum Rock indicated considerable

---

* For example, Title III has funded the Quincy, Illinois, public schools for a $145,000 planning grant to develop "Education by Choice"—a version of Public Schools of Choice—involving 4500 students and over 200 teachers.

community support for educational experimentation and alternative forms of education. For instance, a survey showed that 56 percent of the parents felt that schools should try new ideas, while 74 percent of the teachers and 78 percent of the administrators felt that experimentation, including experimentation with alternatives, was a good thing.

On March 8, 1972, the Alum Rock School Board authorized the superintendent to develop a transitional voucher demonstration. After revision, the proposal specified:

> . . . Parents in the attendance areas of the six pilot school districts will receive vouchers worth about $680 for children in kindergarten through sixth grade and about $970 for those in seventh and eighth grades. This amount represents the current average cost of educating a child in the Alum Rock School District.
>
> . . . Each of the six principals (program managers) with their staff will develop two or more alternative, distinct education programs. The programs will operate simultaneously in one or more buildings. The alternatives will be developed with the full cooperation of the community. Efforts also will be made to encourage private organizations and parent and other public groups to develop programs that would be operated under contract with the public school board.*

The Alum Rock transition model differs structurally from the original voucher model in essentially four ways:

1. The EVA [Educational Voucher Administration] will function as an advisory board to the school board rather than as an autonomous, publicly constituted body.
2. Interested new school groups will have to contract with the school board to become eligible for voucher funds, rather than apply to the EVA for certification.
3. Six schools and approximately 4,000 students will participate in the first year of operation, rather than the original expected 12,000 to 15,000 pupils.
4. Each of the six schools will offer at least two alternative programs rather than one.

* *A Proposed Demonstration in Education Vouchers*, Office of Economic Opportunity, Office of Planning, Research, and Evaluation, Pamphlet 3400–8, April 1972, pp. 16–17.

Further, the Alum Rock school district has committed itself to expansion during the second year if the demonstration is successful; if not, the project will be phased.out.*

Philanthropic foundations are always on the lookout for new ideas, especially if their money can be used as "seed" or "transition" money for reform. The Ford Foundation, for example, was the first to provide planning money to both Philadelphia for its "school without walls," and to Berkeley for its "alternative schools project." The Ford Foundation continues to support educational alternatives by funding public school systems moving toward diversity. In announcing its grant to the New York City Board of Education for "mini-schools" at Haaren High School in Manhattan, the Ford Foundation noted:

The operation of sixteen mini-schools at Haaren High School during the coming year will be assisted. The mini-schools range from specialized programs in aerospace and automotive training to broad college-bound and pre-technical curricula. They are based on voluntary participation by teachers and students, and follow a strategy recently adopted by the Board of Education to introduce more personalized teaching patterns into the city's large high schools.†

We must find new ways of looking at the problem of financing. Certainly, more money is needed to update so massive and strategic a network as our public schools. As national and state priorities change, education will, we feel, be the recipient of increased revenues. However, public schools already have enormous resources at their disposal, and these can be distributed in new ways to help solve some of our basic educational problems.

It may seem an oversimplification to argue that we can launch a new system of public education tomorrow by merely rearranging existing ingredients. However, that is indeed possible. Re-

---

* *Ibid.,* pp. 20–21.

† *News from the Ford Foundation,* Thursday, December 30, 1971, p. 4. See also pp. 125–26 above.

member, this plan rests entirely on choice, and lack of money is not a major obstacle. Attitude, awareness and intent are the true problems.

Granted that public schools can utilize existing resources differently, and that small sums of "new" money can be used for conversion to an alternatives framework, what are other implications of this plan?

VIII / IMPLICATIONS OF PUBLIC SCHOOLS OF CHOICE

As with any other reform proposal, Public Schools of Choice raises important questions unrelated to financing. Some such questions are raised with genuine concern for the possible impact an internal voucher approach might have on some of our cherished ideals—on integration, for example. Other questions have a different tone—they ask whether or not the implications have been thought through.

Obviously, our proposal would have important implications for literally every dimension of the public school system. As an example, whereas at present public school supervisory personnel use their time and energy in one way, implementation of a Public Schools of Choice system would certainly cause them to work in quite another way. Briefly, supervisors now spend most of their energy trying to improve the standard educational process so that it can serve more learners. They are trying to make *one alternative*—the existing school program—work for all children. But, as we have noted, this effort has had limited results. We are

223

not here blaming the supervisor for a poor job; on the contrary, many supervisors work round-the-clock to accomplish the tasks assigned them. Rather, our point is that the task is literally impossible and so results in frustration for both the supervisors and their clients.

Public Schools of Choice would redefine the supervisor's role: Instead of being engaged exclusively in improving .the existing program, he would assist in the development of a range of legitimate alternatives. Other roles would be redefined as educational options were developed. With a range of different educational environments available, the school psychologist, for instance, could help learners connect with that environment which would best serve the learner's aspirations, the one most congruent with the learner's style of learning. Such a framework would enable a new type of "diagnosis and prescription" to take hold—one in which teacher style and learner style are more closely matched. The support staff would not have to assume the role of trying in one way or another to influence the learner to adjust to the standard school process, if that process were not working for the learner, but would provide opportunities for the learner to become aware of, and have access to, other educational options.

In that situation, educational personnel would be more likely to view school problems not as a "student-fault" phenomenon ("he simply cannot adjust to the school"), but as the result of the choice of a "wrong" educational alternative for the student. The attitude that student failure is more likely a function of a mismatch of learner to educational environment than the result of lack of effort or ability can go a long way toward humanizing the process of schooling.

Public Schools of Choice would certainly contribute a great deal to "humanizing our schools." The entire structure of the plan is based on recognition of the rights of individuals. The important point here is that the goal of humanizing our schools is not limited to one group only—the students, for example—but extends to teachers, parents and administrators as well.

At present, it must be recalled, alternatives may be developed by teachers, or parents, or students, and then imposed on the other groups in the name of "humanistic education." For example, some well-intentioned teachers and administrators have developed "open classrooms." They have developed these as a step in the direction of humanizing the schools—yet, they have, in some cases, simply imposed this style of teaching on children and their parents, whether these consumers wanted it or not, whether the children could learn from it or not. Public Schools of Choice is humanistic not only in its product, but also in its process.

Other major areas too will certainly be affected by Public Schools of Choice: minority interests, including the problems of desegregation; the preparation of educational personnel, especially teachers; the role of private schools in this country; and the status of the profession itself. Let us consider each of these areas in turn.

DESEGREGATION

Would Public Schools of Choice really benefit the minorities who have been shortchanged by public schools? How would Black, Puerto Rican, Chicano and Indian groups view this plan? Would not Public Schools of Choice work against racial desegregation?

Since the 1954 Supreme Court decision, considerable effort toward integration has been based on the assumption that the achievement of Negro pupils would be enhanced in an integrated school environment. Minority communities, realizing the importance of education to their individual and group survival, have often resorted to measures of desperation. They have sought alternative paths to quality education: control of the public schools or escape to parallel private schools.

Faced with an increasingly defensive public school bureaucracy, many parents and community leaders have called for decentralization and community control, rather than integration. This is especially the case in our big city school systems. In New York City and Detroit, for instance, city school districts have been decentralized into community school districts, each with its local governing board. The hope in these urban districts is to increase the responsiveness of the school to the community it is designed to serve to the end that improved learning may result.

In other cities, minority communities have established private community schools. The Federation of Community Schools, in the inner city of Milwaukee, is composed of seven member schools, which serve about 2300 elementary students. The Federation is designed to:

1. remain completely independent in all areas of the decision-making process so that each school would respond in its own ways to the cultural and educational needs of the community in which it functions;
2. work together to discuss mutual problems and coordinate common services and resources.*

In most large cities, the "minority" school population is now the majority. In almost all the communities which have called for greater community control, the schools are almost totally black, Puerto Rican or Chicano. The primary concern in these communities now is to achieve "quality education." Increasingly, communities have "given up" on desegregation as the primary vehicle for achieving this. They have waited too long. Promises of desegregation have been followed only by tokenism

* Booklet, The Federation of Independent Community Schools, Milwaukee, Wisconsin.

—especially in the North. Thus priority continues to be given to quality education.

Harlem Prep in New York City has broken new ground as a virtually all-black high school, in that quality education is there actually being achieved. For example, black graduates from Harlem Prep and from other schools like it now enter the nation's top colleges as this description emphasizes:

Students spend at least a year at Harlem Prep, during which time they generally improve their reading comprehension by at least two years. Most of the students are from 17 to 21 years old and, reflecting the community served, are black. Harlem Prep aims to not only provide young blacks with a high school education but to enable them to enter college. More than 700 colleges are now accepting Harlem graduates, who have entered such institutions as Harvard, Amherst, and Wesleyan, McSarlane said. He added that three students who graduated from Harlem Prep in 1968 and went on to complete their college education have now returned to the school as faculty members. Five parents and the student body president serve on the school's board of trustees.*

Other urban schools, in contrast, maintain desegregation as a condition of operation. Parkway in Philadelphia has established racial desegregation through its admissions procedure—a representative lottery.†

An important point to establish is that while integration—a united society—is a goal, the reality is that many, if not most, minority communities live in "neighborhoods" of their own and have schools which reflect that fact. These communities cannot sit by waiting for desegregation to achieve quality education for them. They must improve the education of minority schools.

* From *Alternative Schools: Pioneering Districts Create Options for Students*, Publication of the National School Public Relations Association, 1972, p. 27.

† John Bremer and Michael von Moschzisker, *The School Without Walls*. Holt, Rinehart and Winston, 1971, p. 15.

They have little choice. The late Whitney Young, former National Director of the Urban League, put it this way:

It has also been charged that community control would perpetuate segregation, but we've never had integration and so long as black children are denied decent schools, and black families remain imprisoned in rotting tenements and grinding poverty, agreements about segregation take on an aspect of unreality. The fact remains that the overwhelming majority of black people live in racial ghettos, and giving them control over their lives and their own communities may break the cycle of degradation and powerlessness that crushes so many.*

Public Schools of Choice goes beyond community control by offering *each* individual minority member increased options for achieving quality education. Alternatives can be established in schools which have community control, as well as in those that do not. Public Schools of Choice continues to emphasize *parent decision-making*. It provides increased chances for developing educational environments that are responsive to the style and culture of the community. If one educational option does not work, there are others—so that neither the parent nor the child needs to feel that there is something wrong with either of them.

But, in fact, Public Schools of Choice enhances the opportunities to develop integrated education. Many an educational alternative will find a beginning as an alternative school apart from ongoing schools; and may begin as a new school, either in a separate building, or as a school within an existing school, and then attract an integrated student body.

The Parkway Program, for example, began as an educational unit outside the mainstream public schools of Philadelphia. Students, teachers, parents, who volunteered to enter this "school without walls" all accepted one of its conditions—integration. Since this school used the city as its classrooms, there was no

* Whitney M. Young, Jr., *The Journal of Negro Education*, Vol. XXXVIII, No. 3, Summer, 1969, p. 290.

segregated school building. Since learners met at different institutions in the city, away from neighborhood schools, there were more chances for integration.

Further, educational alternatives can be based on a newer conception of integration—multicultural education, which establishes cultural diversity as its founding principle.

Public Schools of Choice can help reduce the tensions and conflict which seem to be built into the conventional desegregated school—especially at the secondary school level. The causes for racial confrontations are complex, but they can be dealt with, at least in part, by creating a framework in which students have access to classes and programs that are tied to their own concerns. Black and white students who work together to plan relevant instructional programs may gain a new sense of connection in the process. Then learning takes top priority, not interpersonal conflict.

Many feel that integration is more a psychological than a physical state. They see that physical mixing is not the same as integration—that a sense of self-worth and equality are more essential. Some minority communities prefer to have their own public schools—even when these are perceived as segregated. There are predominantly black schools which emphasize racial solidarity (for example, Black House in Berkeley). Some Spanish-speaking and Oriental minorities are doing the same thing. Options help these groups as well.

PRIVATE SCHOOLS

If there is a crisis in public education, there is most assuredly one also in private education in this country. Rising costs have taken an unusual toll of private schools, especially parochial schools dependent exclusively on tuition. Attempts to secure public support for some private schools have run head-on into the issue of separation of church and state.

Yet private schools have always played an important role in American education. President Nixon made clear how the private schools serve the needs of the nation when in April 1970 he appointed the President's Panel on Nonpublic Schools:

Nonpublic elementary and secondary schools have long been an integral part of the nation's educational establishment . . . They provide a diversity which our educational system would otherwise lack. They give a spur of competition to the public school through which educational innovations come. Both systems benefit, and progress results.

Should any single school system, public or private, ever acquire a complete monopoly over the education of our children, the result would neither be good for that school system nor good for the country.

The nonpublic schools also give parents the opportunity to send children to a school of their own choice and of their own religious denomination. They offer a wider range of possibilities for educational experimentation and special opportunities, notably for Spanish-speaking Americans and black Americans.

There is an equally important consideration; these schools—nonsectarian, Catholic, Jewish, Protestant and other—often add a dimension of spiritual value to education, affirming in children a moral code by which to live. No government can be indifferent to the collapse of such schools.*

Private schools have been used as an option by 15 percent of the school population of the nation. For those Americans who were economically advantaged, private schools have long served as an escape-route from public schools, which had the mission of educating everyone. As a result, many private schools early took on an "exclusive" flavor. For other Americans, parochial schools offered a choice they preferred to secular public schools.

In some European countries—the Netherlands, Belgium and Denmark—the government has established a voucher system in which the parent may choose either a public or a private school. With public schools increasingly unsatisfactory to Calvinists, Roman Catholics, and Dutch Reformed parents who preferred

* The President's Panel on Nonpublic Schools, April, 1970.

strong religious training for their children, a steady exodus from public schools has occurred since 1857, the year when parents gained the legal right to establish their own schools. Between 1880 and 1950, the proportion of elementary schools that were public schools dropped from 71 percent to 34 percent.

In the United States, many private schools, including some now considered "religious," can become "alternatives" within a Public Schools of Choice structure, as can certain private schools which have emerged as a result of serious shortcomings in the public schools. Harlem Prep in New York has taken the casualties (the dropouts) of the public schools and turned them into high school graduates qualifying for some of America's finest colleges. But Harlem Prep has had to depend on outside support for funding, since most of its students are poor; the school would find it difficult, if not impossible, to charge tuition as a major means of financing.

However, if Harlem Prep can retain its uniqueness as an alternative *within* Public Schools of Choice, why should it not be funded and continue as such? At this moment, the school is faced with continuing fiscal problems. But as a legitimate alternative within a Public Schools of Choice organization, it would receive fiscal support from the public purse. (The students at Harlem Prep are entitled to some support, anyway.)

In a proposal developed by the Committee of Community Schools in New York City, six independent schools—Children's Community Workshop, Discovery Room, East Harlem Block Schools, Harlem Prep, Leap School and Lorillard—described as "quasi-public schools"—would become "independent public schools."

This proposal calls for the creation of a new organization whose purpose will be to find regular public education funding for independent, community-run public schools. This organization will be called the Committee of Community Schools.

The activities of the Committee of Community Schools will be guided by the theory, based in law, that community schools are essentially public schools. In other words, as tuition-free, nonsectarian, open-to-all educational institutions, the members of the Committee and other community schools fall within the statutory definition of "public schools." The Committee's name for community schools which fall within this statutory definition is independent public schools. We call them independent public schools rather than simply public schools in order to suggest the new administrative relationships which need to be established to integrate community schools into the public school system.

The program described in the following pages outlines alternative ways in which independent public schools can receive public funds, as public schools, without jeopardizing the integrity upon which the independent public schools movement is based.

The Committee will present ideas of its members, and of other independent public schools which wish to participate, to the principal sources of regular education monies: the City, the State, and in some cases, the Federal Government.

In its presentations the Committee will delineate as firmly as possible the means by which public funds may be legally transferred to independent public schools.

Further, the Committee will seek to enlarge its strength, and the strength of independent public schools in general, by consulting with schools on the availability of public funds and the means by which they may be obtained. Under the existing system, public money goes to both the public and the non-public schools. While the members of the Committee are currently classified as non-public schools, because we are privately, rather than publicly, supported, we basically operate like public schools without public funding. As a consequence, independent public schools end up being neither clearly public nor clearly nonpublic, but, rather, quasi-public schools, a situation which results in financial aid from neither side.*

Enabling legislation that would allow "independent" schools to become public schools was introduced in the New York State Legislature in 1972. An act to amend the education law entitled "Independent Public Schools" proposed the development of

* Committee of Community Schools, *Progress Report*, December 4, 1971.

parent-controlled alternative schools within the public school system. Under the proposed legislation, a qualifying school must maintain at least 150 pupils and have the written approval of the local school board. While this particular piece of legislation was not enacted in 1972, its introduction does appear to provide a "preview of coming attractions."

Parochial schools can similarly qualify as public schools, if direct religious teaching takes place only after public school hours. To be sure, there might be sticky problems associated with this, but parochial schools have also changed over the years. They have, for instance, more lay teachers nowadays. Further, our experience with Title I of the Elementary and Secondary Education Act, in which parochial and public schools cooperated, has already developed common ties between the systems.

Certainly, we should explore the implications of this movement further—in the spirit in which options and choice have been offered. What is envisioned is an expanded, broadened conception of public education in the United States—one that enables a wide range of alternatives to exist within its framework. Parochial schools, for instance, have had to assume a competitive, almost antagonistic, economic and political stance vis-à-vis the public schools. Energies which could have been coordinated on the national problem of delivering quality education were fragmented and used to "fight" one another. A redefined system of *public* education, one that encourages alternatives, could bring an end to this "tug of war," while also maximizing family choice.

PREPARATION OF EDUCATIONAL PERSONNEL

Public Schools of Choice affects the preparation of educational personnel very directly. At the present time, teachers, administrators, counselors and school psychologists are usually prepared within the "monolithic structure" of public schools. That is, the public school itself is the laboratory which prepares its teachers. Future teachers and teachers on-the-job are learning the ways of the existing institution: that is how the role of the teacher is formulated. Thus, teacher preparation institutions depend on public schools to teach student teachers their roles. Students in training observe, participate and practice-teach in standard public schools.

Indeed it has been thought desirable for teachers in training to deal with the realities of public school life, and this too has strengthened the dependence of teacher-training institutions on standard public elementary and secondary schools. Where student teachers were placed in schools that diverged from the uniform patterns, they ran into trouble later as beginning teachers, for their philosophies clashed with those of the schools which employed them. Both the new teacher and the employer suffered in these cases. At times, teacher-preparation institutions which tried to give prospective teachers an awareness of other patterns of education (for example, of progressive education) were viewed as "ivory towers," removed from the realities of public schooling.

Indeed, the "reality" was, and still is, largely the monolithic public school system. Future teachers learned the ways of the standard school—first, as students from kindergarten through high school, and then as student teachers.

The fundamental point here is that *the public school trains the teacher; the environment of the public school shapes the behavior of those within it—new and old teachers alike—as it does that of all other educational personnel.*

Only now something has begun to change. Public schools are being criticized for failing with ever-increasing numbers of learners. Can this be because teachers-in-training are learning only the ways of the established school—that teachers are not learning other ways?

As students, parents and teachers demand alternatives, teacher-preparation institutions will begin—very slowly—to be responsive to their demands. Public School alternatives, where they exist, provide opportunities to prepare teachers for diverse educational processes. Both pre- and in-service teachers have a new opportunity to develop their own styles of teaching and to cultivate those styles in educational environments that are supportive.

Such educational environments are beginning to be found in the public schools. We now have teacher-preparation institutions geared to "open classrooms," to "behavior modification," to "multiculture," for example.

As public schools offer more alternatives, *these alternatives become the setting for the training of teachers.* Already teacher-education programs are in operation that emphasize close connection with alternative schools. These include programs at Indiana University, at the University of Massachusetts at Amherst, at Mankato State College in Minnesota, and at the University of Vermont.

Over fifty undergraduate and graduate students are enrolled in the new Alternative Schools Training Program at the School of Education, Indiana University. This field-based program has sites in alternative public schools in Bloomington and Hammond, Indiana; Grand Rapids, Michigan; Louisville, Kentucky; and Seattle, Washington.

Other teachers' colleges involved with the preparation of personnel for alternative schools include Virginia Polytechnic Institute; University of Vermont; and University of North Colorado, Greeley.*

Furthermore, alternative patterns for becoming a teacher will

* *Alternate Schools*, p. 46.

also emerge. Consider the following proposal made to the Fleischmann Commission in New York:

DEVELOPMENT OF ALTERNATIVE TEACHER PREPARATION PROGRAMS. To enhance the establishment of a common, performance-based system of certification, we are proposing expansion of the program options available to both student and professional. These are examples of alternative teacher preparation models:

—*Existing sequence:* Two years of general education, followed by two years of professional education concentration, culminating with student teaching.

—*Clinically-oriented sequence:* This model shifts the bulk of teacher training from campus to school. Teacher education students begin work with children as freshmen, increasing exposure through the years as assistant teacher, associate teacher, and, finally, as full-time teacher-student. Professional work is integrated around the clinical experiences of the teaching candidate.

—*Master of Arts in Teaching:* College graduates interested in careers in teaching take the internship route, usually spending one semester on campus in academic work and one or more off campus in a supervised internship.

—*Individualized Programs:* A teacher candidate plans his own tailored program with a team of professors. This sequence may help independent study and technological self-instruction, as well as tap the unique talents of the student (he may want to teach in a correctional institution, for instance).

—*New Careers Development Sequence* (paraprofessional emphasis): In an attempt to expand the opportunities and to help find new talent for careers in teaching (especially among the minorities) and to develop differential levels of competence and responsibilities in the teaching act, we suggest a new career sequence aimed at paraprofessionals, such as these: *teacher aide*—responsibilities range from supervision of recess and lunchtime activities to operating audiovisual equipment; *teacher assistant*—supervision of teacher aides, preparation of materials used in teaching and demonstrations, correction of homework, and assistance to students at home; *teacher associate*—works with small and large groups of students and is a specialist in substantive knowledge; *teacher*—responsibilities for planning and orchestrating various educational environments for children.

—*International Education:* This program prepares students for teaching careers in other countries as well as our own. Major portions of the students' time are spent in other countries, usually in centers set up for this purpose. A strong cross-cultural emphasis is expected from this sequence.*

PROFESSIONAL TEACHER ORGANIZATIONS

One of the most important implications of Public Schools of Choice involves the question of whether as a reform it can prevent what appears to be an inevitable collision between parents and teachers, between the public and the professional.

No change in public schools is possible without the support of teachers. Not only are teachers close enough to learners to influence them emotionally, but also they have the power to bring an entire system to a halt through strikes. Teacher power is one of the major elements in today's education. Yet, a complex of economic, political and racial forces is converging on our public school system, triggering what appears to be an inevitable collision between teachers in their organized professional associations and parents.

The drama which is unfolding in one of America's most sacred institutions has been developing for some time. There are no villains in this drama—just individuals and groups responding to an array of social realities, all of which have begun to convert allies into adversaries. The storm which is forming may be difficult to see in regions where there is still calm and tranquility. However, as with any type of pressure system, it is only a matter of time before new regions are affected. Teachers first joined professional organizations, historical evidence indicates, in order to improve their status, that of "low man" on the bureaucratic totem pole. That was then an intra-institutional struggle. But

* Mario D. Fantini, "The Reform of Teacher Education: A Proposal for New York State." Phi Delta *Kappan*, April 1972, pp. 478–9.

now they find themselves in what appears to them to be an unjust onslaught from without—an attack by parents and legislatures on their well-earned gains of past years. As a result, they are now joining organizations whose main purpose it is to protect their interests and welfare. This they hope to accomplish through group cohesion and political action. These weapons have been potent indeed. They can, as we have said, bring an entire educational system to a halt through a strike.

Teachers are becoming aware of the implications of the new forces surrounding them, sensing that they must continue to build political leverage. This means moving from local and state affiliations to national ones, and from several national organizations such as the National Education Association and the American Federation of Teachers, to a single one that might be an American Teachers Association not unlike the American Medical Association and the American Dental Association in the health professions. Negotiations to merge the National Education Association with the American Federation of Teachers are under way. One thing that is helping this movement toward teacher power is the emergence of a number of politically alert figures within the organizations.

Ironically, the thrust of new political activity will be directed at the educational consumers themselves: parents and students. Parents and students do not have the benefit of the organizational capabilities of teachers, but they do have access to elected officials and can put tremendous pressure on them—indeed, they have already begun to do so, for a variety of reasons. Their voices have led the call for public accountability. The public is beginning to raise serious questions about what the school is or is not doing. There are no villains in this scenario—only people who are justifiably concerned about the direction education in America should take. Who is to decide that direction? What will the costs be? It may be difficult to accept the position that blame cannot be leveled at any one group.

For some of us, the roots of this battle can be found in the nature of the public school itself. We have an institution formed in the nineteenth century which still retains many of the objectives and much of the structure of that era. Yet now it is expected to respond to the needs and values of twentieth century America in all its cultural diversity, and including the premium Americans now set on quality education for all.

A pluralistic culture converging on the school has resulted in the formation of a critical mass of discontented educational consumers who are expecting the school and its educational process to be much more responsive to their unique interests and style than it has hitherto been. This critical mass of dissatisfied customers are expressing their discontent in a manner that is shaking the foundations of public education.

To further compound the problem, a variety of Americans are responding negatively to spiraling educational costs, especially because the financing of public education is so dependent on the local property taxes. We have reached a stage in which, even though they may value quality education for their children, many citizens are forced by the fiscal structure itself to respond negatively to public school demands—to defeat local bond issues, for example. And since the largest item in the budget of any public school system is teachers' salaries, economic pressures on parents are motivating them to examine the schools in new ways.

Faced with economic crisis, parents are beginning to raise questions about teachers' salaries, tenure, and so on. Tight economics becomes the conditioner. It makes parents more "tuned-in" to all other types of school criticism. During the current period of high criticism of public schools, parents are more likely than ever to be responsive to public school failure rates, to student discontent, to student calls for relevance and to the need for humanizing the educational process. All of these begin to take on increased importance when they appear in a framework of economic concern. Increased numbers of parents want, need, expect, quality education, but feel that they are not getting it. They feel that school costs are skyrocketing astronomically and that something must be done about it. These discontented educational consumers, at one time, would have taken the option of sending their children to private schools. However, the spiraling costs of these restrict the private school option for many, forcing them to live with the public schools—forcing them, that is, to live with both high cost and basic discontent.

In the urban centers, this story is almost classical. Parents and students alike are protesting with as much furor as a powerless group can, the inequities of their education. Black Americans have been sentenced to depressed areas and to institutional racism. As victims, they are caught in a cycle of despair: poor education leading to poor jobs, poor jobs to poor housing, poor housing to psychological and social discontent.

Where the casualties are the greatest, so is the retaliation. Parent and community boycotts, calls for community control of schools, have now followed a decade of neglect, of unfulfilled promises, of dependence upon those who are in a position of responsibility, usually white, to improve the lot for minorities, usually black. Such plans as compensatory education and desegregation have proved disappointing. Time has run out. The forces shaping society do not wait for the schools to reform themselves. The cycle of despair grows even more dramatic, the dissatisfaction so much the more pronounced. The call for increased voice in public school governance on the part of minority parents is, naturally, very threatening to those inside the schools, the teachers and administrators. Putting the establishment of educational policies at the community level into the hands of angry minority parents may well cause teachers to feel pressured as they are being evaluated, hired, fired. Such moves are naturally resisted by professional educators. And while it may be natural for teacher organizations to meet such policies with resistance, resistance also naturally leads to teacher-parent conflict.

Dissatisfied customers, looking for more efficiency at lower cost, begin to put pressure on legislatures for such reforms as "performance contracting,"—arrangements in which the local school boards contract with business and industrial firms for the delivery of educational services with moneyback guarantees. Performance contracting too has met with considerable resistance on the part of the professional educators, especially from teacher organizations.

We are rapidly reaching a stage in which the professional educator appears to be "fighting" for his very life. Obviously, if the public really reaches the point where it supports such plans as performance contracting and external vouchers, organized professionals cannot sit by and watch their welfare compromised. Moreover, professional organizations do indeed find much that is substantively wrong with such "desperation" efforts at reform.

Teacher organizations see the threat of such new plans as a ploy to bring about the demise of the public educational system and the people in it. No wonder, then, that many teachers and their leaders have begun very systematically to plan a response to what they perceive as a growing attempt to reduce their well-earned gains. They feel that there is still time, if they stick together, to do something about such threats. This "sticking together" is the key. There is increased realization that teachers must unite, that a new NEA-AFT must now put aside any philosophical differences that they may have had to face together the common threat. What is likely to happen is that, faced with these outside demands, the teacher organizations will become defensive, on the grounds that they are being victimized. It is not inconceivable that the ultimate weapon of the nationwide strike will be utilized to dissipate what appears to be a rising storm of public discontent. It is clear that the public cannot do without education, even the kind of education that costs more than the public would like to pay, or the kind that really does not deliver all the educational services the public would like. Nonetheless only denial of formal education through the closing of schools, perhaps statewide, perhaps even, conceivably, nationwide, can make the public realize the situation. Such a move cannot, of course, be contemplated until teachers are united in one national federation.

Teacher organizations believe that if they had nationwide power, they would use it to reform the entire educational system of the nation; they would use their power, they say, for better education. It is difficult to see how parents, needing and wanting schooling for their children, can accept this strategy. Other factors have surfaced, too: the teacher shortage of the past decades has ended; we now have a teacher surplus. Professional ranks are not easy to keep closed during periods in which people are hungry and "hustling" for jobs.

Policymakers cannot long survive if the drama we have sketched here actually unfolds. They have already begun to set in motion "get-tough-on-education" policies, from cutting school costs to proposals aimed at renewing public education itself. As indicated, the President of the United States clearly enunciated a new reform policy in his 1970 Education Message to Congress. As a result, the terms now most employed in the United States Office of Education are "reform," "renewal," "redesign."

The implications of these policies for current public school procedures will be significant. Professional educators have not been insensitive to the new public demands on our schools. For instance, they have tried to be responsive to problems of educating the poor by mounting programs of compensation. When the crisis in urban education was spotlighted in the 1960's, the professional educators did respond with programs of remediation for the poor (mostly minorities). But now the new policies will turn abruptly from the add-on, compensatory approaches of the past, which have had professional support, to seek new methods of achieving quality education, which may well disturb the professionals. Similarly, in the past, the public schools have responded to societal demands with such reforms as vocational education, adult education, early childhood education, special education of various sorts. Now, however, this add-on strategy will no longer work. Not only are the costs high, but the results are questionable, as President Nixon reported in his 1970 Message to Congress.

Thus while compensatory and add-on programs have in the past been the measures least threatening to professionals, these have now been classified by *public* policy as unacceptable—as only "more-of-the-same."

And the threat to professional educators continues to grow. For example, many minority parents, dissatisfied with the productivity of their schools, now feel they would like different leadership patterns. They want to rely more heavily on black and other minority-group professionals to create educational programs that are more responsive to their needs. In so doing, they threaten directly the many white principals and supervisors in the schools. Given such tensions, teachers and other professional educators turn even more militantly to their professional organizations and to strong leadership within these organizations. Teachers, too, want to feel secure, and they have few options except to count on the strength of their professional organizations to protect them in times of crisis.

For teachers who have attempted to play by the ground rules set by the institution itself, it is difficult to accept and contend with the demands associated with the new wave of public accountability, demands which to many teachers appear unreasonable. The view from inside the educational institution is altogether different from that of the parents outside. To many teachers, being a "good citizen" inside the educational institution means closing the classroom door and doing one's best with a group of twenty-five to thirty-five different children. Not having been prepared by their own education to deal with the problems of cultural diversity, teachers have had to "make it" on their own in the schools. They have had to learn on the job. But they have also learned the ways of the job. They have come to accept the norms of the school. To many, what the school does is legitimate, what creates difficulties and discontent is the increase in the number of students who present problems—students who do not adjust, who have "changed," who are not willing to work as others once did. By these criticisms, teachers really mean that at one time students came to school accepting whatever the school had to offer. It was then the responsibility of the student to adjust to the school. Today, it seems to be the other way around; the school must change to adjust to the student. This is a different, more demanding orientation.

In the past, the student who did not adjust, who did not keep up with the "standards" of the school, had at least the "option" of dropping out and going into the world of work. Today this is hardly possible. More people have to remain in school for longer periods of time to qualify for the demands of our advanced technological marketplace. Further, to flood the labor market with millions of young people would be disastrous to the economy.

At one time, if a child were not responding to the standard public school program, it seemed natural to place him in a classroom for slow children—never mind the stigma! Labor needs of past decades triggered the development of a whole wing of public education called "Vocational Education," which, to many, represented a place for "those who could work with their hands and not with their heads." It was natural to assume that since certain children were "making it" and others were not, those who were not making it were "deviant"; they were "failures." We began to classify human beings as "slow," "underachievers," "disruptive," or "disadvantaged." But as we have said repeatedly in this book, a way of classifying human beings is a way of thinking about them and such classification of students triggers a whole psychology of expectations and self-fulfilling prophecies. The common institutional ground rules have now come to function badly for all parties: for the students who have to adjust to uniformity and conformity, often even against the thrust of their own individual needs and potential; for parents, whose aspirations are thwarted by seeing their children "turned off" or "failing"—by having to accept the verdict that there is something wrong with the children, rather than with the school; for teachers and other professionals in the school who are increasingly the victims of consumer discontent and of institutional outmodedness. To those who worked inside it as professionals, the institution has dealt the most ironic blow. Trying to live by the rules of the institution has resulted in their being used as "scapegoats" for the "system" itself and all its shortcomings.

At the individual school level, the teacher does his best to deal with diversity, individual or cultural, by attempting to "individualize instruction." One of the basic difficulties teachers encounter in individualizing instruction is class size. This concern has reached the teacher organizations, who constantly negotiate districtwide for reductions in class size—from 35 to 33, from 33 to 32, from 32 to 30, etc. Naturally, this approach is expensive, and reducing class size becomes an abrasive proposal to a public already overtaxed. The teachers then argue, "If you want quality education, you have to pay for it." The parents, in their turn, argue: "We can't accept your recommendation. Find other ways."

Standard public school structure compels professional educators to come to grips with the problems of diversity by labeling and classifying children. Often the label used is "disruptive," and it is applied, in most cities, chiefly to minority-group children—thereby creating further bitterness among minority communities and triggering, in turn, demands that authority to label and judge be withheld from professional educators. And so the battle grows. Professionals inside an "old" institution find it natural to propose "old" approaches to the problem. New public policies call for "new" approaches. The public is increasingly complaining that the old policies—reducing class size, offering compensatory education—have, in fact, only made life easier for the teacher, but have offered little "payoff" to the student. These old assumptions as to ways to improve education, however natural they may appear to those inside the standard institution, are now being challenged not only by the consumer, but by many professionals as well.

Here are the conclusions of a study undertaken by one of the profession's most prestigious bodies, the Council on Basic Education, on one of today's major educational problems—reading in inner-city schools:

Reading achievement in the early grades in almost all inner-city schools is both relatively and absolutely low. This project has identified four notable exceptions. Their success shows that the failure in beginning reading, typical of inner-city schools, is the fault not of the children or their background—but of the schools. None of the successes was achieved overnight; they required from three to nine years. The factors that seem to account for the success of the four schools are strong leadership, high expectations, good atmosphere, strong emphases on reading, additional reading personnel, use of phonics, individualization and careful evaluation of pupil progress. On the other hand, some characteristics often thought of as important to school improvement were *not* essential to the success of the four schools: small class size, achievement grouping, high quality of teaching, school personnel of the same ethnic background as the pupils, preschool education, and outstanding physical facilities.*

Decentralization and community control give the voice of the consumer more leverage through elections to the local neighbor-

* Taken from *Summary of Conclusions*, Study from the Council on Basic Education, p. 30.

hood boards. This represents a "get tough" attitude toward professional domination. In some urban areas, community participation has led to new forms of accountability in which neighborhood boards are beginning to develop policies as to the hiring, transfer and dismissal of teachers who are "not productive with our children." Though the new pressures are viewed as unreasonable by professionals inside the educational system trying to make it work, such emerging signals alert the teacher organizations to assume a different stance with their constituencies.

The two different worlds of parents and teachers make it "natural" for them to end up on opposite sides of the problem. It seems inevitable also that parents and the public will eventually win this "war." Teachers may win a few battles, but ultimately, as the saying goes, they will "lose the war." Public education is too vital to the interests of the society itself for the struggle to come out any other way. Public education is the basis on which all societal roles are formed. The quality of our schools determines the quality of life in the community. Schools are the manpower instrument for an advanced technological society. They are tied to the aspirations of societal groups and to individual potentiality. The delivery of educational services must go on, and preferably within the structure of public education. The stakes are indeed high. At risk is not only the future of public education itself, but the whole fabric of American society. The collision we are now headed toward must be avoided at all costs. But can it be avoided? Is it not too late? Can something be done in time? What, indeed, can be done?

The structure of public schools dictates that the energies of all the professionals working inside be aimed at making one, rather monolithic educational process work for everybody. All efforts, whether by teachers, principals, counselors or supervisors, are now aimed at trying to improve the one uniform system. The general prescriptions have been lowering class size, instituting team teaching, using television, introducing the New

Math, new program materials, or in-service training. But all of these are merely attempts to make that one system better; the effort does not come to grips fundamentally with the problems that schools now face: 1) making the school responsive to diversity, to the individual and cultural differences which are converging on the school; and 2) utilizing more effectively the resources that are currently available, rather than always seeking to "add on" to existing resources, always calling for more and more money to do more of the same.

Obviously, we need to open up educational alternatives within the framework of public education, *not by chance, but by choice.* Teachers (and there are a significant number who feel imprisoned by the structure itself) ought to be encouraged to develop alternative forms that are congruent with their own styles of teaching and can offer them greater professional satisfaction and so increase significantly the chances for educational productivity. This is especially likely to occur if the same alternatives offered teachers are made available to students—by *choice.* Such decisions not only increase consumer satisfaction, but also offer new learning opportunities to students who are not responding well to the standard option.

Much more discussion has to take place among professionals concerning the real problem. What is the real problem? The real problem is not that the public is making unreasonable demands, but that the institution in which professionals are forced to work is not, as it stands, capable of responding to the public's demands. The question is not whether to cut off demands, which are in fact justifiable and based on human needs, but rather how to reform the public schools. Professionals must assume major responsibility for this reform—not by adding on layers to a structure which comes out of a different century, but by a re-examination of the problems, and a conversion of the resources that we do have, into educational options available by choice. Alternatives can bring about an alignment of the professional with the educational consumer. Together, their energies can help create an educational structure in which diverse talent and energies can work in a new way—developmentally.

Teacher organizations must use their "power" for leadership, statesmanlike leadership—and that means rising above the environment that now shapes us inside the institution in which we find ourselves. We need a leadership that looks beyond considering class size, reduced pupil-teacher ratios and compensatory education as the only reliable approaches to individualizing instruction and to school improvement—a leadership that will spearhead the opening of options within the framework of public education.

Unless constructive proposals like Public Schools of Choice are acted on soon, collisions between teachers and parents seem almost unavoidable. There is still time now to deal with the common enemy—the restrictive structure of our public schools. Teachers and parents want the same thing—responsive education. The best hope is for teachers and parents to join in the development of educational alternatives within our public schools. Professional teacher organizations can help lead this reform. If they can resist the temptation to protect the existing institution and its conventional wisdom, professional teacher organizations can indeed help parents and teachers to save our schools.

APPENDIX / A LETTER FROM
HERB KOHL

My friend Herb Kohl, in reading the uncorrected proofs of this book, was prompted to write a letter to me. Although his reactions deal with the manuscript in general, his primary focus is on the Berkeley chapter. I welcomed Herb's letter and felt that it should be included in the book for several reasons.

First, Kohl is a recognized author and critic of the American educational system. His views, therefore, are important in their own right. Second, he was one of the pioneer participants in the Berkeley Alternative Schools Plan, serving as the first principal of the Other Ways alternative school. As an involved observer, he has a point of view concerning developments in Berkeley that needs to be considered. Third, Kohl's letter affords the opportunity to update some of the more recent occurrences which, because of publication deadlines, were not included in the original chapter on Berkeley. Finally, this gives me an opportunity to highlight certain interpretations of the book that might differ from those of Kohl.

Dear Mario:

I have just seen the galleys of *Public Schools of Choice* and agree with many of the ideas you presented in the book. We certainly need a wide variety of schools to choose from—as parents, students, and teachers. Coercion should not exist in the context of schooling, if indeed anywhere. Unfortunately, despite the impression that I got from reading your chapter on Berkeley, choice is just what we here in Berkeley do not have. Five years ago a number of people in Berkeley, myself included, decided to fight for alternative schools within the public school system. Our taste was not for private free schools but rather for what you have called "public schools of choice." The beginnings were somewhat as you described—Community High began as a summer arts program and Other Ways as a teacher-training program supported by the Carnegie Corporation of New York. As such, neither of these threatened the school district. As Other Ways moved from teacher training to becoming an autonomous publicly supported junior and senior high school, troubles developed (Community High had its troubles too, but I cannot speak for them). At the end of our first year we asked for public support for our work. The new superintendent, Richard Foster, recommended that we get $50,000 but his cabinet of administrators unanimously opposed him and he went along with their judgment. At that point Other Ways was supposed to accept the judgment of the authorities and disappear. We refused and took our case to the School Board. The result of our presentations to the Board was official recognition as a public high school, a salary for me as principal (which I shared with the rest of the staff, since that was all we had), and the responsibility for finding our own money and facilities.

The same process took place with a number of the other early alternative schools: Kilimanjaro, Odyssey, La Casa de la Raza, Agona. There was deep administrative disapproval, ambiguous support (and occasional opposition) from the superintendent, and eventually support of some sort from the School Board. If not for the Board, there would have been no alternatives in Berkeley. It was not a matter of the administrators or the superintendent initiating new forms of instruction so much as the School Board responding to community pressure. I feel your book hasn't conveyed that, and has left the impression that good ideas will somehow catch the fancy of enlightened administrators and be implemented without struggle.

The idea of public schools of choice did catch on in Berkeley as soon as the idea was coupled with cash—3.5 million dollars' worth of Federal Experimental Schools money. Then it became fashionable to call whatever one had been doing in the past "alternative." Berkeley went through a period of renaming and relabeling. When Experimental Schools Program money became a possibility, the superintendent solicited from the district proposals to be put into a comprehensive document to be sent to Washington for Experimental Schools money. The alternative schools that had struggled for several years were told that their proposals would be considered in the same way as any other proposals that came in. The administration all of a sudden became interested in saying they believed in schools of choice. There were two reasons: one, the money could help the district; two, if everyone believed in alternatives, then the freaks and militants and radicals who struggled for new ways of working with young people were dispensable. As long as everyone was alternative, there was no need to keep us around.

The school district received 55 proposals for alternative schools. Most could be called paint-can proposals—paint the doors of your school purple and orange, choose a hip name, and keep on doing what you have been doing with the students unchanged.

One new school that struggled and managed to survive despite the opposition of the administration was initially even cut out of the proposal. Odyssey, a junior high alternative school, was finally included because many of us, including parents and teachers at the other, already existing alternative schools, put together a collective and fought for each other's survival.

The school district negotiated with Washington for the Experimental Schools Program grant. The superintendent chose as his negotiators precisely those administrators who had opposed the existence of schools of choice all along. When the already existing alternative schools asked for a voice in the negotiations, they were turned down by the local administration and the bureaucrats in Washington. Berkeley got a lot of money to continue failing in the same old ways, using new language.

Some alternatives did survive but the pressure never lifted. Black House and Casa de la Raza have recently been closed down by the Justice Department, which has seen fit not to distinguish between self-determination and segregation. Odyssey has been told that many of its teachers are not likely to be rehired next year by the district. Other Ways no longer exists. I couldn't teach seven hours a day, hassle with the administration another five or six, and then have to worry about survival every summer for more than three years. No one could.

The word in Berkeley is that if you want to do something that can be called open/alternative/nontraditional, then stay away from the so-called experimental schools.

I am a parent with two children in the Berkeley school district. I have no choice—my kids go to the local school. We are in the half of the school district that was designated the control group. I guess the Feds figured some of us had to be forced to have no choice to find out whether choice made sense. The old principal at my kids' school was unsympathetic to any choice. We have a new principal (who came to the school after a lot of struggle by some parents to make the school more open to the needs of our children). The new principal is responsive to the parents, and perhaps we will have a school in a few years where students and parents will have choice—where different learning styles will be accommodated as a matter of course. But this won't come from outside—in fact, it will probably be resisted by the same administrators who co-opted the so-called alternative schools.

What troubles me in your book, Mario, is the trust in administrators, the belief that ideas have power of their own. Ideas are nothing without practice; the ideas only define themselves through praxis—through the commitment and effort to make them work. This practice determined by theory modifies the theory itself so that ideas do not become empty formulas or, worse, vehicles used by people in power to sustain their control over others while pretending to be responsive to people's needs. The Berkeley Unified School District's claim to have schools of choice is no different from Standard Oil's claim that they want to hire revolutionary young men and women to work on their responsive and relevant corporation.

Best,
HERB KOHL

I am grateful that Herb Kohl took time out to forward his reactions to both the book and to the Berkeley chapter. It is important that the reader understand that changes have taken place, indeed, are still taking place, in Berkeley's Alternative Schools program. For example, it is important to note that the Justice Department has temporarily closed two alternative schools, Black House and Casa de la Raza, on the grounds that they were racially segregated. It is also important for Kohl to tell us that the funding for the Experimental Schools Program occasioned a public-relations effort on the part of some of the Berkeley school officials in order to better insure the chances of receiving fiscal support; that in the hurry to qualify for increased support, the original thrust of the alternative schools program was altered; that competition set in, which not only dissipated the distinctive features of certain alternative programs, but substituted polarization for cooperation. However, these developments, while important, are not Herb Kohl's major concern. Herb is after something much more basic.

As a radical reformer, impatient with the pace with which fundamental change is achieved, Kohl has concluded that the educational administrators have succeeded once again in co-opting a plan and transforming it to suit their vested interests. As a radical reformer, Kohl has notions of educational alternatives that naturally differ from those whose inclination may not be radical. This would include, I suspect, most of the school administrators, whose function it is to represent the concerns of a diverse population such as exists in the Berkeley community. By definition, Herb's concept of *fundamental reform* would be radical and, therefore, controversial. In fact, Herb is fond of referring to himself as one of the "crazies." By this he seems to mean that the mainstream interprets his proposals as being too radical or too far on the fringe—the consensus being that anything that is on the fringe borders on lunacy.

Because Herb's orientation is radical, he believes that I am, on one hand, too gentle with school administrators, and, on the other, that I rely too much on abstract ideas. Herb may be right on both counts, but for reasons that I think differ from his own.

The purpose of my book is to present a reasonable and constructive plan for reform of public education—one that is within our reach. Its intent is to bring people together. It is a plan that respects the rights of professional and layman alike. It comes on the heels of a decade of criticism of public education, and after a string of reform defeats. I was involved in many of these reforms, some with Herb, some without. For example, we both participated in the school-decentralization effort in New York City, and earlier in some of the desegregation and compensatory education efforts. I spent six years with the Ford Foundation, dealing with the problems of innovation and change. One cannot go through all of these experiences without having learned important lessons. Among these are that reform proposals cannot be carried through by being shoved down people's throats, that people have a right to differ, and, basically, that the "enemies" of reform are not school administrators, teachers, parents, or any one group, but the outdated institutional arrangements that literally force these groups to engage in negative political conflict. Reform cannot really take place unless the energies of all parties are directed toward reforming the institutional arrangements. School administrators and professional educators respond the way they do in large measure because the institutional structure compels them to behave in this way. The institution orients them toward thinking about reform in certain ways. They are products of the environment in which they work. As a reformer and educator, I must understand the forces that are shaping the behavior of people. Just as I must understand why children behave as they do, and why I cannot "write off" children because they don't fit some preconceived pedagogical notion—on the same grounds, I cannot "write off" adults who are also being shaped by the institutional environment in which they function and whose outlook may differ from mine. Neither can I fault people who become defensive when their personal security is threatened.

In the end, I suppose it is easy to say that Herb and I differ on means and not ends. We both want responsive and equitable education for all learners. Since we don't have this at the present time, Herb is impatient and would opt for a radical, if not a revolutionary, approach to change. This implies struggle and confrontation. I still believe that we can speed up the evolutionary process. I realize that 60 percent of the people whose children go to public schools are satisfied with the type of education they are receiving. They have a right to it, whatever their reasons. Moreover, because they are a majority, they are the gatekeepers of public education.

What *Public Schools of Choice* is all about is attempting to legitimize the rights of all people, not only the 60 percent. However, in my opinion, this cannot be done by telling the 60 percent that their brand of education is stale or inferior. Neither can I expect that the 60 percent who see things one way can be expected immediately to welcome with open arms concepts of education that appear radical. In fact, if *Public Schools of Choice* were viewed as a forum for controversial educational options, then the plan would be politically naïve.

It is likely that the first generation of educational options may be characterized by the lack of "controversial" programs, as Herb suggests. However, it is also likely that as people catch on to the notion of educational options and choice, more so-called "fringe" alternatives will be legitimized.

Initially, perhaps, priority needs to be given to having the idea of public schools of choice understood and accepted instead of insisting that radical proposals be implemented immediately. Actually, reports from various quarters of the nation—if not from Berkeley—are promising in terms of the range of diversity in educational options that have already been implemented without major conflicts—e.g., Shanti in Hartford, St. Paul Open School in Minneapolis.

The fundamental reform therefore suggested in *Public Schools of Choice* is not so much in terms of whether radical groups can find their particular notions accepted immediately within the framework of *public* education; it is, rather, for the mainstream of our society— the major users of our public schools and determiners of their policies —to accept *options* and *choice* as basic rights for parents, students, and teachers. If this idea should click, as I believe it will, then the foundations for altering the institutional arrangements that now restrict us will have been basically reformed.

As I indicated, not every alternative is legitimate. Naturally I don't know all of the intricate politics that took place in Berkeley, and Herb may be right in his analysis. However, Herb is also suggesting that there really are *no* alternatives in Berkeley—that is, no alternatives that may satisfy *his* criteria. It is unfortunate that Kohl and the other professional educators in Berkeley had a parting of the ways. One of the real hopes in Berkeley was that a new framework in public education could develop that would satisfy a diversity of distinctive options, including those advocated by Kohl.

Since no reform is possible without politics, we are forced into an arena which can degenerate into open confrontation. It is difficult for me to see how this will enhance the growth and development of people. Rather, as I have indicated, I am proposing a plan that brings people together. If there is a politics in *Public Schools of Choice,* it is a politics of cooperation. My appeal is to the thousands of people of good will, both in and out of our public schools, who are really motivated by what is best for children. It may appear to be a naïve proposal that a plan can become a rallying point for people of good will; that teachers, students, parents, administrators can work together if they feel that their own rights are not being preempted—but that is my position. Therefore, *Public Schools of Choice* is a hopeful proposal during a period of growing pessimism. The mood of the period in which we now live, coming as it does after a period of struggle and conflict, leads one to hope that most citizens would embrace a proposal such as *Public Schools of Choice,* which appeals to their instinct of fairness and reasonableness. It may very well be one of the final proposals we can make that will enable the various groups to come together. I am aware of the historical tradition in which reforms are diluted and finally disappear in the smothering embrace of the educational establishment; yet, *Public Schools of Choice* comes at a time when there could be a new awakening. The majority of the American people may be tired of disruptive and negative political confrontation. They may find a proposal that has something for everyone refreshing and worthy of serious support. If public schools of choice take the route that Kohl feels has taken place in Berkeley, then it is not far-fetched to conclude that human polarization will reach epidemic proportions—the consequences of which should be clear to us all.